The Complete Guide to Neuro-Linguistic Programming in 2019

How to Use NLP to Overcome Your Fears and Master Psychology, Emotional Intelligence, Stress Management and Ethical Manipulation

Written by Louis Sinclair

© Copyright 2019 Louis Sinclair - All rights reserved.

The content contained within this book may not be reproduced, duplicated or transmitted without direct written permission from the author or the publisher.

Under no circumstances will any blame or legal responsibility be held against the publisher, or author, for any damages, reparation, or monetary loss due to the information contained within this book. Either directly or indirectly.

Legal Notice:

This book is copyright protected. This book is only for personal use. You cannot amend, distribute, sell, use, quote or paraphrase any part, or the content within this book, without the consent of the author or publisher.

Disclaimer Notice:

Please note the information contained within this document is for educational and entertainment purposes only. All effort has been executed to present accurate, up to date, and reliable, complete information. No warranties of any kind are declared or implied. Readers acknowledge that the author is not engaging in the rendering of legal, financial, medical or professional advice. The content within this book has been derived from various sources. Please consult a licensed professional before attempting any techniques outlined in this book.

By reading this document, the reader agrees that under no circumstances is the author responsible for any losses, direct or indirect, which are incurred as a result of the use of information contained within this document, including, but not limited to, — errors, omissions, or inaccuracies.

Table Of Contents

Introduction 14

Principles of Neuro-Linguistic Programming 20

Chapter 1: Emotional Intelligence 23

Neuro-linguistic programming techniques for developing emotional intelligence 25

    Awareness 26

    Motivation 27

    Self-regulation 28

    Empathy 29

    Effective communication 30

Chapter 2: Resolving Anxiety and Negative Feelings 33

Development of anxiety and depression 37

    Compounded challenges 37

    Dissociation from pleasure 39

    Getting stuck in the past 40

    Negative self-talk 41

    Psychomotor retardation 42

Fighting depression and anxiety 43

Chapter 3: Conflict Resolution............ 48

Counseling 50

Negotiation 51

Conflict resolution through neuro-linguistic programming 52
- ☐ Conflict dissociation 52
- ☐ Individual dissociation 52
- ☐ Creating rapport 53
- ☐ Identify and interrupt patterns 54
- ☐ Identify intentions 55
- ☐ Understand different perspectives 55
- ☐ Stages of conflict resolution 55
- ☐ Determine the source of the conflict 56
- ☐ Overlook the conflict incident 57
- ☐ Suggest solutions 58
- ☐ Identify feasible solutions 58
- ☐ Settle the conflict 59

Chapter 4: Managing and Overcoming Phobia and Trauma 60

Neuro-linguistic programming techniques for managing phobia 61

Procedure 67

Chapter 5: Changing Beliefs, Attitudes and Behaviors 70

Understanding beliefs 71

Presuppositions of neuro-linguistic programming 73

Appreciating difference in beliefs and perspectives 75

Communication and responses 77

The role of feedback in beliefs 78

Reframing beliefs and attitudes 81

Chapter 6: Public Speaking and Presentation 83

Why do people struggle with public speaking? 84

Common public speaking challenges 88
- ☐ The audience walks out 88
- ☐ A jeering audience 89
- ☐ Interruptions 90
- ☐ Technical failure 91

- ☐ An unruly audience 91
- ☐ Having nothing to say 92
- ☐ Running out of content 93
- ☐ Running out of time 94
- ☐ Zero enthusiasm 94
- ☐ Repeating a speech 95

Improve public speaking through neuro-linguistic programming 95

  Manage your breathing 96

  Try to relax 96

  Organization 97

  Congruency..98

  The desire for perfection 99

Chapter 7: Leadership and Management Skills 101

Importance of neuro-linguistic programming in leadership 102

  Riding a rough tide.................................... 103

  Beating the competition 104

  Leadership vs. Ruling............................... 105

  Workforce morale 107

  Procedure 108

Passion in leadership 111

Effective communication 113

Chapter 8: Effective Listening Techniques 114

Understand your audience 115

Active Listening 116

Careful choice of words 118

Non-verbal cues 120

Positivity 122

Chapter 9: Managing Stress Through Neuro-Linguistic Programming 124

- ☐ Completing tasks 127
- ☐ Goal setting 128
- ☐ Managing change 128
- ☐ Motivation 129

Neuro-linguistic programming for stress management 129

Reframing 132

Sub-modality alteration 136

Relaxation anchoring (Trance) 137

Chapter 10: Creating an Enabling and Motivational Environment for Teamwork 140

Reasons for Demotivation 141
- ☐ Uncertainty 142
- ☐ Poor Management 143
- ☐ Insecurity 144
- ☐ Lack of Progress 145
- ☐ Leadership Integrity 146
- ☐ Poor Communication 146
- ☐ Unfruitful Partnerships 147

Role of neuro-linguistic programming in the workplace 148
- ☐ Managing Workplace Stress 149
- ☐ Right of Way 149
- ☐ Handling Processes 150
- ☐ Establishing Cooperative Independence 151

Departmental benefits of neuro-linguistic programming 152
- ☐ Healthcare 153
- ☐ Sales 153

- ☐ Education.. 154
- ☐ Welfare Service..................................... 154
- ☐ Management... 155

Improving teamwork through neuro-linguistic programming 155
- ☐ Asking for help..................................... 156
- ☐ Division of labor 156
- ☐ Speaking up 157
- ☐ Evaluation and review 157
- ☐ Winning together................................ 157

Chapter 11: Establishing Quality Relationships 160

How does communication become a problem? 161
- ☐ Language concerns 161
- ☐ Generalized assumption 163
- ☐ Evasive communication 165
- ☐ Invalidation 166

The role of neuro-linguistic programming in creating quality relationships 169

Mirroring and Matching 170

- Physical Mirroring 171
- Kinesthetic Language 172

Important communication lessons from neuro-linguistic programming 173
- ☐ Communication is mandatory 174
- ☐ Yours isn't the only perspective 175
- ☐ Response determines value in communication 176
- ☐ Communication is a resource-based skill 178
- ☐ You are in control 179
- ☐ Separating people from behaviors 180

Chapter 12: Ethical Manipulation in Neuro-Linguistic Programming 182

- Control over thoughts 183
- Perceptions 185
- Techniques used in mind control 185
- Focusing on the individual 186
- Suggestive frequency 187
- Voice roll 187
- Anchoring 187
- Creating rapport 188

Using specific words 188

Subconscious mind programming 189

Chapter 13: Setting and Meeting Goals. 190

What are goals? 191

Positivity in goal setting 194

Specificity 195

Goal evaluation 196

Maintenance 196

Contextualize your goals 197

Resource allocation 198

Goal setting through neuro-linguistic programming 199

Importance of brainstorming in goal setting 201

Chapter 14: Challenges and Limitations of Neuro-Linguistic Programming 203

Hypothetical Observations 204

Lack of Awareness 205

Terminology 205

Manipulation 207

Lack of Growth 208

Clinical Value 209

Need for Intention 210
Limited academic research 211

Conclusion 213

Introduction

Neuro-linguistic programming (NLP) is a technique that was created early in the 1970s by Richard Bandler and Dr. John Grinder. They created a modeling process that allows them to study what makes hypnotherapists effective in their training methods. The study of neuro-linguistic programming is a powerful discipline, given that it has aspects of modern psychology that many people have found useful in most inter-personal and personal relations.

Neuro-linguistic programming is recommended for people who are interested in personal or professional development. There are many cues you learn about effective communication that make the difference between success and failure in customer services, especially for salespeople. Through neuro-linguistic programming, you learn how to improve your awareness of yourself, those around you, and your environment. You learn to listen to your body and the messages that it conveys.

Neuro-linguistic programming gives you a better approach to understanding how people feel, their behaviors, and beliefs, and in the process improving your cooperation and empathy with them. It is difficult for most people to understand what others think or feel, given that they barely understand what they personally feel.

Often, you will come across people talking about emotional intelligence, of which neuro-linguistic programming is an enabling tool. Emotional intelligence is something that most people need to help them foster stronger and better relations with the people they work with. Emotional intelligence is basically what makes you human. No one is immune to sentiments or feelings. It is the way you interpret the feelings and expressions that make other people feel comfortable talking to you or not.

Learning neuro-linguistic programming is a life-changing experience, one that most people would benefit from. The techniques that you learn in neuro-linguistic programming are useful in many situations, and for people in different roles and capacities at work, including the following:

- Administrators
- Receptionists
- Managers
- Directors
- Executives
- Secretaries
- Trainers
- Counselors

Other than the work environment, neuro-linguistic programming will also come in handy for you at home. The techniques you learn can help you improve your relationships with friends and family members. Many relationships have failed because one partner felt like they were being taken for granted. Neuro-linguistic programming teaches you how to be empathetic towards someone else's feelings. Before that, however, you learn how to show yourself empathy. You cannot learn how to care for someone when you do not know what it feels like, or when someone needs care.

Learning neuro-linguistic programming techniques will be useful for people engaging in different circumstances, and will improve the relations and interactions with your audiences. Through neuro-linguistic programming, you learn how to create and define strategies, and set realistic goals.

For people in a managerial or coaching role, neuro-linguistic programming empowers you with the skills necessary to teach your team how to appreciate their contribution, which in the long run fosters greater participation, and since they are satisfied with their work, helps you achieve your organizational goals.

Neuro-linguistic programming is useful in conflict management and resolution. Conflict is a part of life. We cannot live without conflict, because it is a manifestation of two factions whose perspectives do not align. People hold strong reservations for things that they believe in. When these beliefs are challenged, it can be difficult for them to process, and as such, conflict arises. Conflict situations can boil over and become a disaster if they are not managed properly. With neuro-linguistic programming, you learn how to nip such situations in the bud.

Neuro-linguistic programming will also teach you how to build your sales performance and foster great customer relationships. Customers usually move on from one company to another because, amongst other things, they feel their needs are not being addressed. Most sales representatives are focused on bombarding customers with news and information about their products, without stopping to ask what the customer wants. How does the product affect the customer's life? What are the changes in the customer's life and how does this align with product placement goals?

One thing that you will come to appreciate about neuro-linguistic programming is that you learn to take a step back and look at things from someone else's perspective. A lot of times we are conceited to see the world only in the way that we are used to it. Most people do this and lock themselves up in a world where only they exist. Without allowing people into your world, it is difficult for them to understand what you feel or how you see things.

In neuro-linguistic programming, you learn to appreciate the fact that you are different from every other person you come across. Whether at work, at home, or when you are catching up with your friends, you are all different. Everyone has a unique perspective on life, based on their experiences, the way they grew up, their environment, the interactions they have, and so many other factors. These differences are not a bad thing. The differences are what make them who they are.

Through neuro-linguistic programming, you will learn how to be effective in whatever you do, which translates to profitability and productivity on many different levels.

Principles of Neuro-Linguistic Programming

Neuro-linguistic programming is primarily about behavior change and aligning operational philosophies to the said changes. There are different techniques that are available for use in neuro-linguistic programming. The following are the principles that guide neuro-linguistic programming, which you will learn in detail as you look at the different spheres of life where neuro-linguistic programming is applicable:

- Achieving outcomes – This is about determining what you set out to achieve.

- Sensory awareness – Sensory awareness

teaches you about acuity. With the right understanding, you know whether you are moving away from or towards your desired outcome.

- Behavioral flexibility – As mentioned earlier, neuro-linguistic programming is about behavior change. You become aware of your inherent behavior, and change it for the better. You will learn how to modify your behaviors to suit your desired outcome until you meet your goals.

- Working on plans – Since you already have plans, the best time to act on them is right away.

Outcomes or targets must be specific. A lot of people fail to achieve their targets because they are not conscious about what they are working towards, and in the process, they end up struggling and wandering through their lives. Neuro-linguistic programming is specific about having a purpose because a specific purpose guides your actions.

You learn how to speak and act in a certain manner. Neuro-linguistic programming also teaches you a number of behavioral and linguistic patterns that are very effective in helping you learn to change your behaviors and beliefs towards other people and influencing the way they respond to the same.

Above everything else, neuro-linguistic programming is about managing change. You determine the change you want, plan for it, and work your way towards it. Read on to find out how you can use neuro-linguistic programming in different aspects of your life, to achieve greatness.

Chapter 1: Emotional Intelligence

Emotional intelligence is one of the most sought-after forms of human intelligence. It is a set of competencies that allow you to be aware of your emotions and how they change, with respect to your environment and the people around you. Emotional intelligence is about managing your moods, and in the process learning how to use them to do things differently. It also means you must be your own motivator, using resources at your disposal to understand others, and what they feel and communicate effectively with them.

It is very easy to talk about emotional intelligence, but unfortunately, most people cannot portray it. Even the most educated of individuals in society fail when it comes to emotional intelligence. The lack of empathy often ends up becoming a stumbling block to effective communication. Over the years, neuro-linguistic programming has been used in personal and professional development as a means of life coaching and executive coaching. In these coaching routines, you learn how to improve your life, create a sustainable balance between work and your personal life.

Going by the set of skills that you need to learn in emotional intelligence, this is not something that you may or may not have, but abilities that we all have in us. You just need to realize it, become aware of those around you, and learn how to interact with them better. There are three possibilities in emotional intelligence; you are either highly developed, in between, or poorly developed. In the simplest terms, emotional intelligence is about people skills, being in touch with yourself, those around you, and what they feel.

Many are the times when you come across experts in different fields who, however good they are at what they do, barely succeed because they cannot relate well with people around them. We are social beings, and getting along with people is an important part of success in life. You should be able to communicate with people, motivate, and interact with them. You learn how to identify and respond to their impulses and moods.

Without proper emotional intelligence, you will struggle to establish lasting relationships, even social and personal relationships. If you cannot motivate yourself or engage others actively in a conversation, people will shy away from you, and avoid you.

Neuro-linguistic programming techniques for developing emotional intelligence

Emotional intelligence is a product of what goes on in your mind. It has been extensively studied in neuroscience, especially about what happens in the brain when you are going through mood swings. There are many benefits, especially in terms of social interaction, that are associated with emotional intelligence, as applies to neuro-linguistic programming. Mastering emotional intelligence allows you to improve your performance in different aspects of your life, such as education, relationships, and leadership.

As you learn the different aspects of emotional intelligence, you will also learn how to map your core competencies and improve on what you already know. The most important thing about emotional intelligence is awareness.

Awareness

Self-awareness is an important aspect of emotional intelligence. You learn how your brain is running your life, or how you are running your brain. In self-awareness, you learn why some things are more important to you than others. Once you understand this, you will appreciate the things you believe in better, and help you figure out why you behave the way you do or believe in the things you do.

Self-awareness teaches you to dig deep and

understand why you have a strong personal conviction to certain things, why you are drawn to them and not others. With this knowledge, you will also appreciate why you are different from others around you. If you can understand what goes on in your head, you will know that people are different, and others respond to situations differently because of the environments they grew up in, or circumstances in their lives that are responsible for who they are presently.

Motivation

What values do you espouse, and do they drive you towards your goals or not? Motivation is often about the things that you hold dear, the ones that mean so much to you. Once you understand what works for you, you can turn your life around, because you will no longer depend on other people to motivate you or control your life through their expectations, but instead motivate yourself.

Motivation is also not just about you, but those

around you too. In neuro-linguistic programming, you learn how to identify the things that are important to the people you interact with. Based on this information, you can also influence their actions, and use the common values to motivate them to do things and become better. This helps if you are in charge of a team, as you will work towards achieving team objectives.

Self-regulation

How well can you manage your moods? Are you the type of person who has no control over their moods? Being in control of your moods increases awareness, not just for your moods, but also for the moods of the people you work with. You can learn to identify when someone is not in the right frame of mind because you know the cues to look for. You have witnessed the cues in yourself, and learned how to handle them, so it is easier for you to do the same for others.

Empathy

One aspect of emotional intelligence that goes a long way is empathy. By understanding yourself, it is easier for you to understand others too. How do you recognize what they are going through? Can you identify someone who is in pain without them telling you? Let's assume you cannot, what would you do if they came to you and told you about their situation? Do you give them time off? Do you offer solace and consolation? Do you just ignore and tell them to get back to work because everyone has gone through something similar at some point?

Understanding people is not always the easiest thing to do, but it is possible, and one of the best things you can learn in neuro-linguistic programming. It opens your eyes, and you see life the way other people see it. You put yourself in their shoes and experience their lives with them. This is one of the best people skills you can learn, and it increases the trust and confidence that people have in you.

Most people worry about showing empathy because it is one of the easiest sentiments to be abused. That being said, however, does not mean that you should not show it. The more you learn about empathy, the easier it will be for you to tell genuine cases from fake ones.

Effective communication

Communicating with people is only effective if you can understand each other. One of the tenets of emotional intelligence requires that you learn how to speak to people in such a way that they do not feel you are talking at them. You need to foster healthy communication lines between individuals and groups, to make sure that each participant's point of view gets respected.

Communication is also about learning behavior patterns and how they affect people you interact with, and how their behavior patterns affect you. One of the skills you should master is using specific questions instead of issuing statements. Statements can appear to be overbearing over the audience, but a question brings them into focus and attempts to get their perspective of the situation.

Communication also teaches the importance of learning useful interpersonal skills. This is an art that will help you gain trust amongst those you interact with, and encourage them to feel confident in talking to you about the things that concern them.

With these techniques, you can make several changes in life, especially about how you relate to those you interact with on a daily basis. Remember, however, that situations might not always be the same. Before you introduce the theoretical approach to emotional intelligence or neuro-linguistic programming, you must realize the real-life situation you are in and appreciate the fact that situations are not always the same. Some techniques will work all the time in most cases, others will work in specific cases. Whatever you do, do not treat anyone you interact with as a case study, but handle situations on a person-to-person basis. You must be genuine in your show of emotional intelligence, lest you be accused of manipulation.

Chapter 2: Resolving Anxiety and Negative Feelings

Anxiety does not just affect the individual, but those around them too. Through neuro-linguistic programming, it is possible to help individuals overcome anxiety. When you are around someone who is constantly worried or frightened about things that most people do not worry about, it can affect your life in a dramatic way.

In the simplest terms, neuro-linguistic programming is a tool that helps you develop flexible behavior, in the process becoming competent at what you do. Whether verbally spoken or not, there is always a conversation, or communication in place whenever socialization takes place. There are so many things that people are afraid of, some which are obvious and others that you might not think about until someone opens up to you. Why is it that people are afraid of the things they are? The simplest explanation for this is that it depends on how their brains interpret the signals in response to these things, and how it processes that information.

Anxiety will often graduate into irrational thoughts, and from here you will experience symptoms like a racing heartbeat, stomach ache, profuse sweating, and so forth. The symptoms are not the same in every person. More often, by the time someone gets anxious to the point where their body is showing physical symptoms, they can barely point out the specific reason why they are in the situation they find themselves in.

Anxiety bouts often leave the individual feeling depressed, nervous, and inadequate. This lowers morale and makes you feel very low about yourself. Most of the time, people who suffer anxiety attacks tend to be low on self-confidence and avoid interacting with other people as much as they can.

Neuro-linguistic programming is about language, the brain, and programming. It has proven to be effective in the past in managing anxiety. Neuro-linguistic programming is so efficient, it can even work on children. What neuro-linguistic programming does is to identify the dynamics between language and your mind, and how the relationship between these two affects your behavior patterns and your body. Through neuro-linguistic programming, you can regain your confidence and manage stress better. It will also help you reduce the feeling of guilt you experience each time anxiety sets in, and over time, you will not worry about the negative thoughts that you have struggled with.

Depression and anxiety are things that are not usually discussed often, but given some of the high-profile deaths that have happened in the past, people are opening up to have candid discussions about depression. According to relevant statistics, depression is currently one of the leading reasons why people ask for days off from work – taking over from persistent back pain.

Most GPs are recording insane traffic in terms of people who come in to discuss depression and anxiety. There is a lot of misery going around to the point where you stop and wonder when we lost the plot. When did life become so bleak? Why is it that a lot of people are going about their lives in so much misery and pain? Something has to be done to change this outlook because if young kids who are barely in their teenage years are taking their lives out of depression, we need to find a solution.

For most patients, antidepressants are useful and have helped them deal with depression and anxiety. However, these can fall short in supply, and there is the risk of addiction and overdose. A better alternative to antidepressants is learning useful techniques that will help patients feel better by the time they are leaving the consultation room.

Through neuro-linguistic programming, you learn to impart positive emotions to the individual, like calm, happiness, and warmth.

Neuro-linguistic programming further enhances an interpersonal approach to psychotherapy that makes the patient feel at ease and comfortable around you. By learning neuro-linguistic programming, you become aware of skills that enhance the relationships with people around you who might be struggling with anxiety, and you can make a big difference in their lives.

Development of anxiety and depression

There are distinct emotional stages that an individual goes through when they are depressed. It is from these stages that the mind picks and locks on to the negative emotions and pessimistic perception of life that patients portray.

Compounded challenges

While someone might possess a predisposition to negativity out of experiences that they have had in life, their depression can be kicked into motion by a single moment in their day. Take the example of someone who just received a regret letter from a company in lieu of an opening they had applied for. If the person has a pervasive approach to life, they would blame themselves, wondering why they are not good enough for the position. On the other hand, someone with a positive outlook would perhaps think the interviewing panel did not understand why they were good enough for that role, or perhaps they did not allow themselves sufficient time to prepare for the interview.

Someone who suffers with depression will always deal with situations in their lives in a pervasive manner. They always look at life in terms of the problems that befall them. Such individuals, therefore, end up compounding their challenges, and their thoughts are filled with universal quantifiers. While neuro-linguistic programming can help such individuals change their outlook, it is not about making them believe or think life is a wonderful bed of roses. Experts warn that any attempt at hoodwinking such individuals in this manner would leave them susceptible to harm in the event that they encounter a similar situation.

One of the concerns that depressed people have is the tendency to compound their desired outcome when they go for therapy. Successful therapy is not about setting standards that are unattainable, but about determining the difference between what might happen and what has happened.

Dissociation from pleasure

There is a big difference between a happy person and a depressed person's cognitive function. Happy people have a lot of pleasant memories in their minds, which are very easy to recall. The reverse is true for depressed people. While a happy individual will see pleasant memories to be significant in their lives and very real, depressed people see unpleasant experiences as their normal state.

Most of the time, a depressed person will only relate to problems. It is not easy for them to draw positive experiences or solutions, and even if you share this with them, they find it difficult to believe these experiences happen in people's lives. Through neuro-linguistic programming, you learn skills that teach you how to dissociate from the negative unpleasant experiences and have a positive outlook on life. In their minds, a depressed person is often afraid that such changes are interfering with the reality of their lives, which is misery, and consider happiness an unreal sentiment.

Getting stuck in the past

For the brain to constantly revolve in a pervasive state, the individual will have certain memories of their past that they cannot let go of. Most people who are depressed are always stuck in something that happened a while ago. This is slightly different from what anxiety does to a person because anxiety creates worry about something that is to happen in the future. Anxiety is also an impulse-related reaction because the individual is worried about what happens in the present moment, and how it will affect their future.

Depressed individuals see the present and the future from one point of view, the past. Someone could say they are always unhappy because they have never gotten over the death of a loved one. Another example is someone who has a bleak outlook for the future, because of something that someone did to them in their past, and they worry about opening up to someone else, lest they suffer the same fate.

While it might help to discuss the things that happened in the past with the patient, at times this becomes counteractive because it reminds the patient of the reason why they are the way they are. Through neuro-linguistic programming, however, it is advisable that you try to encourage the individual to focus on what the future holds for them.

Negative self-talk

According to neuro-linguistic programming

experts, the amount of emotional trauma you suffer is directly proportional to the amount of negative self-talk you allow yourself to listen to. The feeling of helplessness might happen infrequently, or it might happen frequently. However, the more you think about it, or give it attention, the more it will manifest and become a part of who you are. This is how depression grows.

It starts by the individual feeling uneasy about something, then they talk about their worry that this might become a permanent thing, and they will not be able to overcome it. From there, the individual will feel worse about their life.

Psychomotor retardation

Psychomotor retardation is a state where the depressed person suffers a motor response go-slow. This happens when the individual chooses not to exercise. In the absence of exercise, the individual will soon have to deal with insomnia. Insomnia is an energy-intense experience, and in its wake, the individual will exercise even less than they are supposed to. What most people do not realize is that a brisk walk for a few minutes is enough to improve their mood for more than an hour.

Fighting depression and anxiety

What we see here is a dilemma not just for the depressed individual, but also for the person who is trying to assist. Depression stems from an innate belief that the individual is beyond change. What you learn in neuro-linguistic programming is to encourage the individual that instead of counseling or psychotherapy, what you are doing is consulting with them, as their personal coach. This takes a different approach to the norm.

A depressed individual comes to you to assist them in coming up with a plan of action that will have a positive effect on their lives. You have to remind them often that the road to recovery requires a collaborative effort. Other than following the advice, they also have to assist in coming up with the same.

You must also debunk the myth that you have a magical or miracle formula that will get rid of depression. However, change is inevitable if you follow the guidelines accordingly. Many are those who claim that neuro-linguistic programming does not work for depression, anxiety, and negative thoughts. The problem here is that they have a different approach to what they should. Neuro-linguistic programming helps by explaining how things should be done. It teaches you techniques of how to go about the problem. You have to put in the work.

Consulting the depressed person is important because it helps them become a part of the solution. They feel the difference in progress over time. The following are some questions that you can ask the depressed person, in the hope that they can search deep within for answers to their current predicament:

- What do they expect to change after talking to an expert?

- What do they want to achieve at the end of the session?

- What do they need to see to believe that their problem is solved?

- How do they know that they no longer have a problem?

- If the problem has been solved, what will they feel or do differently than what they used to experience earlier?

- Are there any moments when they feel different when they feel they are okay?

- What happens when they feel different?

- What are they often doing at the time when they feel different?

Neuro-linguistic programming helps the individual at different levels. From identity, beliefs, behavior change, purpose, and their environment, these are the things that are dear to an individual, and this is where neuro-linguistic programming effects change. These are the levels through which neuro-linguistic programming can help an individual change their perspective, become more positive about life, build their confidence, esteem, and motivation. Someone who is shy can learn to become confident in their ability and express their feelings and thoughts in a coherent manner through neuro-linguistic programming.

An anxious person finds it difficult to think rationally. Through neuro-linguistic programming, however, they get emotional support and an understanding of why they experience the feelings they do and learn how to solve the conflicts within themselves. There are many neural pathways that can be used in neuro-linguistic programming alongside linguistic and visual aids. These support features help to strengthen the brain for individuals who struggle with anxiety and depression.

Chapter 3: Conflict Resolution

It is impossible to find a situation in the real world where people are always getting along. Conflict is a part of the interaction process. If you are always in agreement with people around you, chances are high you are not communicating effectively with them. Conflicts can arise for many reasons. Personality disputes, disagreements, external and internal pressure, and different beliefs are some of the reasons why you can end up in a conflict.

In most cases, people respond to conflicts by ignoring the conflicting party altogether. This is often a short-term solution because the issue at hand is not addressed. After a while, the conflict boils over and graduates into something bigger. At that juncture, radical measures must be taken to address the conflict.

Conflict happens everywhere, even at home. It is

not confined to the workplace. You can learn simple neuro-linguistic programming skills to help you manage conflict and diffuse situations, preventing them from getting worse. It takes patience and skill to understand how to manage a conflict. Since there is more than one party involved in a conflict, especially at work, you might need lots of training too.

In any business setup, the human resource teams are taken through training to learn how to handle conflicts. One of the first things that you learn in neuro-linguistic programming is the need to understand the differences that people share. You must improve how you negotiate, communicate, and counsel individuals for you to resolve any conflict. More importantly, you have to be impartial to the disputing parties.

Disputes must not always end in a lose/win situation. Everyone can leave a discussion with a win/win outcome. With the skills you learn in neuro-linguistic programming, this is possible. Here are some important skills that you will learn in neuro-linguistic programming:

Counseling

Before you get to the negotiation table, you must understand what the problem is that is creating conflict. This understanding gives you a starting point in your solution finding approach. In neuro-linguistic programming, you learn how to identify language patterns. Language patterns are not restricted to spoken language because you can also learn so much about someone and their perception of the situation from their body language.

With this knowledge, it is easy for you to turn your communication in such a way that you can address the needs of both parties. In counseling, it is important to make everyone feel you understand their position. This makes it easier for them to open up to you and share their problems and concerns.

Once you have someone's confidence, you can

then proceed to ask precision questions. A precision question is one that elicits a true answer from the recipient. You can only get an honest answer from someone in a conflict when they trust you and are confident that you will not use their answer to put them at a disadvantage.

Negotiation

Communication is important for any effective negotiation to proceed smoothly. Through neuro-linguistic programming, you will learn how to communicate with the warring parties, and get them all to come to the discussion table. You will also learn how to influence the way individuals communicate and think. When you are negotiating a truce in a conflict, you must offer practical solutions that each individual will be happy about. No one wants to come to a negotiation table when they know they will not get anything out of it. More often, you need to make it clear to the conflicting parties that they must both be willing to compromise something, or they risk losing everything.

Conflict resolution through neuro-linguistic programming

Neuro-linguistic programming provides important tools that you can use for conflict resolution. The following are simple tips that will guide you in an attempt to resolve conflict:

- ***Conflict dissociation***

The first step in neuro-linguistic programming when you are addressing a conflict is to dissociate from the conflict. You take the view of a third-party, someone who has no vested interest in the conflict. In this position, you are not emotionally attached to the conflict or either party to it. Conflict dissociation demands that you remove any emotion from the conflict, and instead, observe and learn.

- ***Individual dissociation***

Dissociating from the individual is easier said

than done. You might encounter a situation where the stakes are not the same for everyone. In such a case, there is no win-win situation at play. Instead, one person might have everything to gain while another has everything to lose. Such are situations where there are external features or factors at play.

The important thing here, as you will learn in neuro-linguistic programming, is the need to maximize the prospect of a good result. In some conflicts, you might have personal feelings involved, but you have to learn to shut them out. At the back of your mind, you should focus on the negotiation process, irrespective of what you feel for the person or subject in question.

- *Creating rapport*

For you to succeed in conflict resolution, you must be ready to create rapport between the parties involved. It is wise to match the tone and speed of the conversation in the case of a conflict. However, the challenge is doing that without making the aggrieved party angry. Once you are on the same page, you need to calm the individual down, let them breathe easy, to the point where they are comfortable and talking smoothly. This is a good way of getting a peaceful solution, and it helps because you improve the communication between the two parties.

- ***Identify and interrupt patterns***

Conflicts usually have a pattern. More often, the situation can only get worse than it is when you identify the conflict. What you are supposed to do is to interfere with the pattern, interrupt it and calm down the situation. You can do this by interrupting someone who is angry and shouting at the top of their voice, and telling them it is important that you resolve the issue at hand, but you would need a moment to think things through. You can also promise to take a step back, think about it, and get in touch with them in a few minutes.

- ***Identify intentions***

Whenever there is a conflict, the people involved tend to focus more on the details. At times it is in the details that the conflict takes place. What you need to do is understand what both parties are looking for in the conflict. When you understand that, it is easier for you to come up with a useful strategy that will help them manage the situation well.

- ***Understand different perspectives***

There is never a good time to step into someone else's shoes than when resolving a conflict. When you do this, you get to see things from their perspective, and it changes your idea of the whole situation. This also gives you a chance to feel what they feel about their situation. By changing your perspective, you will learn and feel, see and hear what someone experiences, and this can help you understand the conflict better.

- ***Stages of conflict resolution***

It is easy to say that there are steps to follow in

conflict resolution, but in the real sense, things manifest differently, and the steps might not always work in the same manner. What you try to avoid is poor conflict management. Everyone has a different personality. This means that they look forward to unique goals, and have differing opinions on many subjects. It is impossible that they will all be on the same page all the time.

Managers and supervisors are often trained in conflict management. It is important that people in their position understand how to manage conflicts. These skills make it easier for them to foster professional growth. The following steps should guide you in managing conflict:

- ***Determine the source of the conflict***

The first thing you have to do in the event of a conflict is to identify the source. You need to get as much information as possible about the conflict to know what it is about. With more information, it is easier for you to solve the problem. There are leading questions that you can ask which will help you determine the source of the question, like *when did this start? Do you see a connection between the two incidents? When did you start feeling this way?*

In conflict resolution, you need to allow both parties to share their perspective on the conflict. This will not just help you understand it better, but it also makes them understand that you are impartial in the conflict.

- ***Overlook the conflict incident***

Anger persists in a conflict not because of the issue at hand, but because of different perspectives. Most conflicts occur because both parties are not on the same page, perhaps because of their beliefs. Many negotiators often admit that the source of the conflict barely is as big a problem as the sentiments that they feel towards it. This explains why people end up trading personal barbs against one another. At such a point, the source of the conflict might have manifested so many days, weeks, or even months ago.

- ***Suggest solutions***

Once you have listened to the perspective of both parties, you need to figure out how to assist them. At this point, ask the parties to propose a solution that they feel would resolve their conflict amicably. Since you are a mediator, you need to listen actively and pay attention to the non-verbal cues. Do not disrupt them, just let them speak their minds, and recommend solutions.

The good thing about suggesting solutions is that you will be pushing the two parties away from anger, towards conflict resolution. You will also have succeeded in making them feel they are part of the resolution process.

- ***Identify feasible solutions***

Having listened to the proposals that they made, address the advantages and disadvantages that you see in them. Address this from their unique perspectives, and from the perspective of a neutral party. If at work, address this from the perspective of the company – what the organization stands to benefit from their proposals, and whether it is feasible or not. Cooperation, for example, if used as an option in resolution, would work well for the company.

- ***Settle the conflict***

If you have decided on the best way to solve the conflict, you must make sure the parties are on the same page. Get them to shake hands once they have accepted the proposals you recommended. Where possible, draw up a contract with timelines within which certain actions must be fulfilled. You also should have a plan in place in case the parties do not honor the agreements you made. In this case, ask them what they feel should be the best course of action if they end up with the same problems in the future.

Chapter 4: Managing and Overcoming Phobia and Trauma

The mind uses our senses to decipher information. However, the effect that the information has depends on whether you will dissociate or associate with it. Association takes place through experiences that you can relate to. This is where the senses come in. If upon interacting with this new information, you choose to take a different perspective from what you would consider a norm, you are dissociating from the information. Through dissociation, you respond to the information in the same way a third party would, as an outsider.

The impact of associated experiences is greater than most people are aware of, especially compared to dissociated experiences. Naturally, the body is wired to be attached instead of detachment. This is what makes the difference between enjoying, being in, and feeling the moment, and imagining yourself being there.

It is through the understanding of such differences that neuro-linguistic programming can help you overcome fears and phobias, especially from previous trauma. Through neuro-linguistic programming, patients learn to face up to their phobias by learning to reframe their experiences and dissociating from those which they have been afraid to associate with.

Neuro-linguistic programming techniques for managing phobia

The human brain processes information from an analytical concept, or through experiences. Experiences give you the feeling of being part of a something like you have entered into the scene. This is what you get when you read or think about something. Over time your brain learns to experience things by responding to certain cues.

If you read or think about something from an analytical concept, you treat it with contempt.

You think about it, analyze it to help you understand it better, and form an opinion about it. An analytical perspective is no different from a spectator's perspective. The difference between these two is that in experiences, you learn to associate with the content in your environment, while in an analytical concept, you dissociate with the content.

There are benefits and disadvantages of taking either of these positions to processing information. Association allows you to experience life as the first point of contact. You interact with things in your environment from within. Dissociation, on the other hand, takes a careful approach. Dissociation applies personal analytics or scientific analytics before you can decide on how to respond or react to a situation. In dissociation, your aim is to learn from situations and to make sure that you do not allow them to induce emotional responses.

If you experience content in your environment from too much association, there is a risk of becoming an emotional cripple. You can easily become hysterical and barely think straight. Most of your reactions are emotional. On the other hand, dissociating too much from events can train you to become emotionally incompetent, blocking your ability to relate to events and content at a personal or emotional level, and this can harm your relationships with people around you.

Mirroring this to unpleasant realities and trauma, a lot of people never want to think about or relive their experiences. Doing so puts them in an uncomfortable position where they have to experience the trauma afresh. Over time, such people will lose the fight in them to handle thoughts that they consider painful. It is easy to develop PTSD at this juncture. The reason for this is because the individual finds it almost impossible to do anything without delving into the painful and negative emotional state. Such people end up learning to avoid, deny, and suppress certain thoughts because they are depressing.

Visual kinetic dissociation (V-K dissociation) is a neuro-linguistic programming technique that can help individuals recover from such traumatic events. You learn how to think about the things you once considered unpleasant and traumatic, without re-entering the traumatic experience. Through neuro-linguistic programming, you will learn how to signal your body not to respond to your thoughts as if you were reliving the traumatic experience in real life. In doing so, you will manage the trauma in your life better, and you can learn how to deal with the pain and move on.

The technology used in visual kinetic dissociation moves you conceptually to a different reference point. You get to view the information your brain processes but from a distance. This process keeps you from associating with the experience, and helps you access and understand your emotional state better. As you do this, you have a good chance of introducing new resources into your life, which will help you understand the situation better.

Visual kinetic dissociation moves you to a different reference point (spectator point of view) where you can see the painful experience comfortably. This helps you overcome and interrupt the trauma you are going through. In so doing, you no longer process the traumatic experience in a negative way and prevents you from emotional collapse.

This is a constructive understanding of subjectivity, and the more you learn about it, the more you learn how to identify where your traumatic experience comes from, and how you can relate to it in your mind and body. You learn new experiences, coding the information into your system. Once you learn how to change the coding, you can also change your experience with trauma at a neurological level.

Based on the association and dissociation thought process, you can learn how to be flexible consciously, and choose which thought process to employ at different points in time. You will learn how to code your experience with information differently, by taking emotion out of your experience and addressing your situations analytically.

When faced with old, traumatic events, you will see them as a spectator in a movie, instead of as the main character in the film. This process of managing emotions teaches you to learn from your past traumatic experiences, instead of feeling bad about them. If you feel you cannot handle certain experiences, you can easily turn them off.

While visual kinetic dissociation works for traumatic experiences, experts also warn about using them for pleasant experiences. If you do that, you will learn to dissociate from them, neutralizing them in the process. Neutralizing these events can eliminate emotional understanding, motivation, and the feel-good feeling about life.

Procedure

This process only takes around ten minutes but is very effective. Think about that moment you have dreaded for a long time or that one thing that you are afraid of. If it is a memory you have lived before, try to think about the traumatic impact and feelings. This process should invoke sentiments and reactions that the expert can study, measure and calibrate. It gives a clear picture of your state of mind when you are afraid.

By recognizing your state of fear, it is easier to identify when you are on the edge in the course of therapy, and you can step back. During the moment when you are fully aware of the phobia or your response to fear, you can change the subject abruptly, allowing you to get back to a positive place before you can proceed with the routine.

Close your eyes for a moment. Imagine yourself sitting alone at the movies, staring at the large screen, but instead of your favorite film, you see pictures of yourself doing something that does not invoke any emotional sentiment. This is ideal especially if you visualize memories.

Think of yourself as a ghost, leaving your body and floating away to the projector to a point where you can see yourself at a distance within the audience, looking at a real-life movie of your life. While still in the projector room, turn the movie on and witness the horrific experiences that you have feared for a long time transpire before your eyes.

Watch yourself seated in the theater, watching the movie, and note the reactions. Since you are watching this as a dissociated observer, you have a different perspective of yourself. Once the film runs its course, revert to a neutral image on the screen. Since you have been watching everything in black and white, imagine turning everything into color. Color emphasizes the senses, what you are feeling, hearing, and seeing. Through color, you can associate with the experience you see on the screen.

Try taking a quick glance at the movie again but from the end this time. Instead of watching it again, spend a few seconds reliving the moments of the film in reverse, and note how you feel about the film. When you do this, you should not experience the same effect that the film had on you earlier on, or maybe you do not have the same feelings at all. The idea here is to reframe the horrific sentiments and emotions and neutralize them. This is the process that therapists use. If you are not successful in the first attempt, the second visit to your therapist would involve hypnosis through systematic desensitization.

This is a technique that has been used in neuro-linguistic programming for a long time, and is useful in working through fears and phobia, especially fears that cause panic attacks in the presence of unique stimuli. However, take note that this process is only recommended for mild phobias.

Chapter 5: Changing Beliefs, Attitudes and Behaviors

Humans are habitual creatures. We learn out of habit. Most of the things that we do are the result of consistent learning and practice to the point where they become the norm. In neuro-linguistic programming, the concept is to explore the impact that your beliefs and attitudes have on your life. Neuro-linguistic programming looks at how your beliefs, habits, and attitudes affect your life, how they determine the kind of person you are, and more importantly how you can try out a different way of doing things to see if you can change your life for the better.

Neuro-linguistic programming works in the same way that meditation does with affirmations. If you speak something to your mind and soul for a long time, you believe it is possible, and you find yourself working towards it. As long as you have a strong belief in your ability to do something, you probably will succeed at it. On the other hand, if you do not believe you can do something, even if you try so hard, you will never make it. This is because you have already programmed your mind to believe it is impossible. Therefore, you will be trying to do it out of pressure, reluctance, and apathy, and this will not work.

Understanding beliefs

Why is there so much attention to your beliefs? Why are they important? Beliefs are a construct of the brain. There is no tangible evidence to support their existence. However, they give you a predisposition to behave in a certain manner or to respond the way you do. Beliefs are a natural phenomenon, and everyone has them. You have to believe in something. People will not always believe in the same thing or believe that the other person is right, but they believe in something. Even the most skeptical person alive believes in something.

An interesting feature about believing in something is that it is possible to be deeply involved in your beliefs. Once you form the opinion that your beliefs are true, you will hold onto them irrespective of the impact that they have on your life or those around you. Beliefs can manifest in a selfish way too. You always think about yourself, what you believe in, and what is best for you. It is more of a personal conviction, something you hold dear and in high regard. Most people are deeply offended if someone questions their beliefs. This is how deep people feel about the things they believe in.

In neuro-linguistic programming, you will learn that beliefs manifest in two ways; the construct of the belief, and the implication of believing in it. By design, beliefs are a general concept about something or an individual.

The implication of believing in the personal conviction is the effect that it has on the things you do on a daily basis. It is about how the belief changes or steers your life. It is possible to believe in a lot of things. However, if you feel they do not affect you or others that you are interacting with at a particular moment, then there is no place for them in the discussion you are having. On the other hand, there are people who do not have that level of control over the things they believe in. For such people, any discourse will easily divert into what they feel should be discussed, or how they want the discussion to be driven, to suit what they believe in. Which raises the question, why should you hold onto certain beliefs, even when you know they are negatively affecting the interactions around you, yet you have demonstrated over time that they are not true?

Presuppositions of neuro-linguistic programming

The idea behind helping others through neuro-linguistic programming is that you have to share certain beliefs for you to assist others in the same way. It is the same beliefs that the individuals you are helping will adopt in order for them to change their ways. It is through our senses that we connect to the world each day.

The implications of this connection are not the same, however. Everyone connects to the world from a different perspective, depending on what their mind is perceiving at that moment. To create a good map of the world in our heads, we need to see, hear, and connect to what we feel by filtering less information from what is fed into the mind. A stronger connection through the senses allows us to have a better connection and communication with the rest of the world.

It is from the sensory input that the brain maps memories. By altering some functions of the sensory input, we change the mental images that the brain receives, and in the long run, the experience that we expect from each interaction changes too. Therefore, following this illustration, it is possible to change or boost positive memories in the brain and reduce the impact that negative ones would have. This is how to change beliefs and attitudes.

Appreciating difference in beliefs and perspectives

In neuro-linguistic programming, you learn that what you believe must not always be the same as what someone else believes in. Everyone creates a different illustration of the same thing in their mind, depending on their circumstances. It is through their experiences with the stimuli in question that their minds create filters relative to that moment. Reality is different from what goes on in the brain. You might be looking at or experiencing the same reality with someone, but the way your brains will interpret it is not similar.

When we fail to communicate well with others around us, it does not mean that this is a permanent issue. It is a function of the model of the world that we have in our brain. It is easier to communicate better with people whose brains are aligned in a similar manner to ours, but this is not a predisposition that we can choose. To understand someone better, therefore, you have to first appreciate that they are different, and you accept them as they are. When they acknowledge this appreciation, it is also easier for them to open up and understand you better.

If you come across someone whose perception of the world is nowhere close to yours, it is safer to start from their perspective, understand them and where they are coming from, then you can work your way up to where you are, or a middle ground where you can both understand one another.

Through neuro-linguistic programming, you learn to understand yourself and those around you, and in the process become more aware of the different perspectives that people have of the same thing as you do. This understanding helps you learn how to change the way you perceive reality. Altering a perception is more useful than altering the content relevant to the perception.

In the same way, you understand that it is possible for bad things to happen. You also realize that when bad things happen, you cannot change the content, but you can accept that the content can be dangerous to you. You are in control and can change how you respond or react to the bad situation. You can also change the lessons you get from a bad situation. Neuro-linguistic programming teaches you how to respond to situations, and change your attitude towards them.

Communication and responses

When you communicate with someone, there is a response you are hoping to get from them. If you do not receive this response, you should consider changing the way you communicate with them. Successful communication, therefore, is not based on what you think about the message, but on the way, the recipient responds or reacts to it. This is why if you do not get the response you desire, it is advisable that you change the way you are communicating.

There is nothing different in the recipient's

ability to comprehend the message you are sending. They have all the resources in them already. Your challenge is to find a way to appeal to their senses so that they can respond to your message as you need them to.

More often, if you believe in someone, you expect them to respond to your messages faster and easily. This also changes your perception of them and influences your relations. In such a situation, you have a predisposition to support, encourage, and at times mentor them instead of castigating them. While this is true, people barely change from outside. The best change comes from a deep desire to change from within. It is possible to change someone, but outside influence also disempowers an individual. If you are to empower someone to change, show them you believe in them.

The role of feedback in beliefs

Failure and success are normal aspects of life. No one is perfect. The day you believe you are perfect and cannot make a mistake in life is the day you stop learning, yet learning is a never-ending process until the day you die.

What does feedback have to do with beliefs? Think about a time when you failed at something. Failure opens a path to success. It is the feedback you get from a failed situation that helps you become better. Success is a good thing, but it can also insulate you from feedback, and therein starts your journey to failure.

What you need to do is learn to overcome the fear of failing. Instead of being afraid, learn to come up with a decision-making strategy. Use each moment of failure as a lesson in what you should do better and how. This kind of feedback changes your perspective of life. You will no longer see failure as the end, but a chance at a new beginning. You will take the lessons you learn from failure and use them to aim for greater things.

In life, people view behaviors and beliefs as bad

or good in relation to a specific context where the behavior holds value, and where some result is expected. Through neuro-linguistic programming, therefore, you are not working towards removing what you would consider bad behavior, because some of them are useful in some places. What you will learn to do, through neuro-linguistic programming, is to identify and appreciate useful behaviors and know where they are relevant.

Neuro-linguistic programming teaches you the importance of discovering positivity in intentions and actions behind someone's behavior. If you can see the positivity in someone, it is easier for you to make the best choices about them. When you constantly see the positives in someone, your perception of them changes, and you believe in them.

Through belief, you offer choices to individuals, not trials and dilemmas. You give them opportunities. The problem with dilemmas is that they often force you to choose the lesser of an evil pair. On the other hand, choices and opportunities born out of belief in someone have alternatives.

Reframing beliefs and attitudes

You can use neuro-linguistic programming to reframe beliefs, attitudes, and influence behavior change. This is a simple process that should give you a solution to the challenges you are facing, or show you what you are supposed to do.

You must first acknowledge that you need to change a certain behavior pattern. Identify and be conscious of the fact that you need to change something. In the process, you should be aware of any changes that take place, whether in the mind or in the way your body feels. If the change makes you feel comfortable and confident, you are on the right path.

In neuro-linguistic programming, you will learn that beliefs, attitudes, and habits are not permanent. However strongly you hold onto something you believe in, there is always room for change. You can also only change if you are willing to accept change. You must acknowledge the differences that exist in people's lives and the fact that situations are not the same. It is by accepting these differences that you will be willing to reframe your belief and accept the value of change.

Chapter 6: Public Speaking and Presentation

The fear of public speaking is something most people experience. You find yourself in front of a crowd ready to present your speech, then all of a sudden, your voice fails you. It cracks. Your palms are sweating, your legs can barely keep you up, and in an instant, you wonder why you had to go through with the speech in the first place. You could have easily let someone else give the speech, but here you are!

As a consolation, however, you are not alone in this. An estimated 40% of the world's population struggle with public speaking, and fear it more than death. Public speaking cannot kill you, however. Whether you are in a professional career or not, at some point you will have to make a public speech to an engagement. Even if you are not in a professional career, you can be called upon to make a speech at a wedding, a church, a celebration, and so forth. Some people are so afraid of speeches, they cannot even give a speech in front of their family members.

Talk to anyone about your struggle with public speaking and you can be certain one of the first three responses would be to think of the audience naked. This works for some people, but not all the time. There are many factors that come into play when determining the course of public speaking. Through neuro-linguistic programming, you will learn useful strategies that will help you stop panicking. You do not need to picture people naked all the time.

Why do people struggle with public speaking?

You are simply standing in front of people and making a speech. Often, there is nothing the audience has to do but sit down and listen to you. Why, therefore, are people so afraid of speaking in front of crowds? Anxiety and nausea set in for most people just before they make a speech. Even those who seem to do it so well tend to struggle –

they just don't let everyone know they do. You have to own your presence in front of the crowd. Make your presence felt. The anxiety and nausea you feel just before you make a speech is referred to as glossophobia. Glossophobia can be mild, making you nervous. In some cases, a panic attack might set in and you become so frightened you do not make the speech at all.

A possible explanation for why people are afraid of speaking in front of a mammoth crowd is that the attention gets to you, and you forget that the speech is not about you. The speech is not even about your hair, the clothes you are wearing, or your confidence in front of the crowd. The speech is about the content. The audience is present to learn about what is in the speech. What they need you to do is to present the content in an amicable manner, so that they derive value from it.

You can learn some neuro-linguistic programming strategies that will help you make your speech without worrying about the presentation or stage fright. Other than managing your presence on stage, neuro-linguistic programming can also help you learn how to impress the audience, irrespective of the size. You will learn how to improve your communication skills, become confident, and command the stage.

Neuro-linguistic programming is about awareness. When you are mindfully aware of your approach to public speaking, you will be in control physically and mentally. This is how you learn to alter the perception of public speaking. There are a lot of things that you might have learned about managing nervousness while you are on stage. One of these is to control your voice. It is almost impossible because you are already in an uncomfortable position. If you try to control your voice in such a state, you only end up making things worse. Your thoughts focused on voice control will make your work difficult, and you will not be able to manage your voice mechanisms either. The audience recognizes discomfort, and some audiences might make life more difficult for you instead.

You might also try to speak louder in order to project your voice, and express a feeling of control over the crowd. Increasing your volume in the right way is a good idea. However, since you are nervous and you are not in control, there is a risk that you might increase your voice and only end up making noise while at it. This explains why some people feel a lot of pain after giving a speech. If you exert yourself too much, you will create unnecessary friction which dries the throat and causes a creaking sound.

Instead of taking such an approach that only leaves you worse than when you started, you should think about neuro-linguistic programming. In neuro-linguistic programming, the idea is to create a rapport with the audience, space, and yourself. Once you are in harmony with your body and blend into the environment around you, it is easier to fight all the concerns you might have about public speaking, and deliver an awesome speech.

Common public speaking challenges

Fear is common in public speaking and presentation. Even the best and most eloquent speakers are afraid of something. The following are some of the main challenges that speakers struggle with, that you might relate to:

- ***The audience walks out***

Well, if the entire audience walks out, you are probably doing something wrong. The chances of the entire audience walking out are so rare. However, there is always that one person who feels like they are wasting their time, and they walk out, or a few people walk out. This is a nightmare for any public speaker. At that point, you are not sure if you are the problem, or perhaps they have something pressing they need to attend to – it could even be an emergency.

People will always walk out of a speech, and in most cases, there is nothing you can do about it because it has nothing to do with your speech or yourself. There are many reasons why people stand up and walk out – apart from a well-orchestrated walk-out, so you should learn to ignore the distraction and proceed with your speech.

If you are witty, you can even use the person or people walking out to charm the audience into a pun. This takes the attention off you and creates a light moment, making things easier as you proceed with the speech.

- ***A jeering audience***

What is so bad about jeering? When people are jeering, do not try to speak at them. This will only create a tussle of which one of the two factions is the loudest, and the crowd always wins. You can shout over the microphone all you want, but you cannot beat the crowd to noise.

Jeers are common in public speaking. Even presidents get jeered, but we don't see them giving up. The secret to jeering is to survive. Jeers can destabilize you and get you off track for a while, but you should face it, own it, and come back stronger. Surviving a jeering crowd in public speaking changes you, it makes you bolder.

Think about the reason why your audience is jeering. Reflect on it later on, and figure out what you could have done better. Perhaps they jeered because of something you said, which makes a big difference since the audience might be right. If what you said in the speech is an important part of it which you cannot avoid, you have to accept that jeers will be a necessary evil if you have to give that speech again.

- ***Interruptions***

Don't we just hate them? There is always that one person that keeps interrupting your speech. They keep raising their hands to ask questions or poking holes in your speech. Such people can make you lose the plot, and turn your speech into a confrontation.

The best way to deal with them is to stay calm. Pause and give them a chance to speak up.

Address their concern, and remind them that there is room for questions later. Stress the importance of listening to your speech, and remind them to take notes, then they can ask their questions later. Addressing such interruptions without confrontation is a brilliant idea, and you even feel more confident and in control of the situation.

- ***Technical failure***

Imagine you are out on the podium giving your speech and then, all of a sudden, the PowerPoint slides go blank, or you have a power failure. Technology is awesome, but technology can fail you. It is advisable that you prepare adequately, and factor in this risk. Have manual notes. Besides, when you write your notes, you can add a few cues in there that can help you steer the conversation in whichever direction you want.

- ***An unruly audience***

You might find yourself in a situation where the audience is out of control, and do not want to hear the topic you want to talk about. This happens a lot when you are dealing with learning institutions. The herd mentality can catch you off-guard. If this happens, try and get one of them to come up on stage, and tell you why they are resisting the discussion you want to have.

Chances are high that they will send a representative, and from there, they can listen to you. It is reasonable to be flexible about how you want to handle the discussion, especially if the audience is so vocal about what they want, and if your discussion points are so far away from their expectations.

- ***Having nothing to say***

If you are giving a speech and there are other speakers ahead of you, there is always a risk that someone might cover what you want to talk about. You cannot follow them on stage and repeat what they did. Your audience will be bored. It is wise to know who your fellow speakers are, and what they might talk about.

Other than that, you can also come prepared with a second speech, just in case someone beats you to your discussion. If you must give the same speech, prepare different examples in a way that you will not bore your audience.

- ***Running out of content***

However prepared you are for the speech, it is possible that you might run out of things to say. If this happens, use the audience. You can ask questions and make it an interactive approach. Read your discussion points and consider the amount of time you have for the speech. You can use this to gauge whether you will have enough time, or if you need to be creative.

Some speakers start by making a brief speech, then they engage the audience in a question and answer session, keeping it as interactive and lively as possible, and finally finishing the speech. You can also create small groups in the audience where they interact with one another for a few minutes before the question and answer session begins.

- ***Running out of time***

It is professional courtesy to say all you need to within the allocated time, especially if there are other speakers after you. If you notice time is running out, you need to polish up and end your speech without making it feel like you are leaving something unattended to. Remember that the quality of your speech matters more than the duration.

- ***Zero enthusiasm***

Everyone has one of those off days when you do not feel like giving a speech. Since you already committed to the speech in the first place, you must show up. The audience is already committed to hearing what you have to say. Psyche up and give a very good speech. You never know, some of these speeches might end up lifting your spirits and turning your life around.

- ***Repeating a speech***

Depending on the nature of the audience and the subject matter, you might find yourself in a situation where you have to give the same speech in different places. Remember that your current audience might not have heard the speech before. At the same time, it is also possible that they could have come across it in digital media.

You have to make this speech look and feel fresh. Come up with new examples; use fresh anecdotes to make things different. You have a lot of time to practice the speech. Say it to your team to determine whether they are confident in the examples you are using, or the approach.

Improve public speaking through neuro-linguistic programming

Having looked at some of the challenges that you might experience in public speaking, it is wise to learn some neuro-linguistic programming exercises that will make your life easier whenever you are preparing for a speech.

Manage your breathing

Something as simple as breathing can make a big difference in public speaking. Take a moment and breathe. You will find yourself on stage, afraid and holding your breath. By holding your breath, you are denying the brain oxygen, in the process stopping your thought process. Think of new ideas as new breaths of air. Breathe deep, pace your breaths, and your mind will be clear enough to keep your subconscious confident and relaxed.

Through neuro-linguistic programming, you learn how to move from an undesirable behavior to an awareness position you want. This is a good exercise that you can perform on your own as you prepare for your speeches.

Try to relax

It might not be easy to manage tension when you are on stage, but you need to. Managing tension allows you to relax, feel free, and use your voice properly. You need to engage the audience fully, and you cannot do this when you are tense. Relaxing allows you to breathe without any concerns. You create a situation where your body is moving freely, in the process controlling your presence on stage.

Organization

One of the best ways of overcoming the fear of public speaking is organization. Organize your ideas. Write down the talking points. This makes it easier for you to remember the important parts of the speech and the ones that you need to highlight.

An important part of organization is to manage the introduction to your speech. Managing the introduction helps you reduce fear and anxiety. If you give a good introduction, it is easy to grow into it, and give a good speech. Practicing before you present the speech makes it easy for you to overcome fear and anxiety. As a confident speaker, you can deliver the message to the audience better and captivate them.

Organization also means you need to know the audience ahead of the speech. Understand what their needs are. Study the demographics and know the composition of your audience. This will help you know the appropriate phrases and examples that they can relate to. You can also search online for some recent news items that the audience might relate to, things that will help you drive your points home faster.

Congruency

As the speaker, you have a better knowledge of the content you are about to speak on than anyone in the audience. When you are addressing the audience, this should be evident. Get your points across in a manner that adds value to your audience. Choose your words carefully so that you can express yourself confidently.

However attached you are to the subject you are discussing, do not let your emotions take control. Often, the audience has no idea about your passion for the subject, or how deeply you feel about it. Theirs is to come with a clean slate, anticipate your delivery, and then draw conclusions later on. If you make a mistake while presenting the speech, do not dwell on it. Move along.

If you feel deeply about a subject and you are trying to teach the audience something new, this will be useful. Share this passion in the engagement. The fact that you have been invited to give the speech and not someone else means a lot to this audience, especially if it is in a field of your expertise.

The desire for perfection

This cannot be said any clearer, no one is perfect. It is okay to make a mistake when you are speaking to an audience. You can stutter, use the wrong word in the wrong phrase or even forget what you are supposed to say. These things happen to everyone. When you realize a mistake, stay calm and let it boil over. Some speakers even use such mistakes to stir up the crowd, reminding them that they barely noticed them making a mistake. It can create a light moment that calms down the tension in the room.

Through neuro-linguistic programming, you will learn skills to help you deliver information to an audience confidently. You learn how to get your audience eager to listen to what you are talking about. The idea is to focus on the things you feel positively about, your strengths, instead of the negative sentiments.

Chapter 7: Leadership and Management Skills

Now more than ever, managers need to finetune their leadership skills. The business environment is so dynamic, and you need to perform at your peak to get the best out of your employees. This is what sets apart the best managers from poor performing managers. In management, you can only ever be as good as the team you are handling. In your capacity, you must be a motivator, inspiring, managing, and fostering effective communication in your team. You should also be the ultimate coach.

Through neuro-linguistic programming, you will learn how to develop skills that will help you manage the team properly. One thing that is important in this case is behavioral flexibility. You need to allow yourself room for improvement, at the same time appreciating the unique differences that make every member of your team who they are. A team is composed of different minds, different individuals with unique abilities. To enhance their performance, you must consider the nature of the complex relationships that exist in the group, and how they influence the cross-functional relationships.

Another issue that you must address in leadership at work is how to manage stress. There are lots of stress factors in the workplace. These come from the desire to meet deadlines, and work within constrained budgets, amongst other things. It is not easy for everyone to handle stress in the same way. Some people will buckle under the pressure, others will manage just fine. The overall responsibility rests on the team leader, however.

Importance of neuro-linguistic programming in leadership

There is a lot that you will learn about neuro-linguistic programming, especially when you attend seminars. You learn from other managers and leaders you interact with, and you will also learn from some of your team members who have had an experience with neuro-linguistic programming at some point in time. The following are some of the takeaways that you can look forward to when you learn the neuro-linguistic programming techniques:

Riding a rough tide

The business environment is turbulent. Companies are resizing, closing down, struggling to make it in a market that is ever so competitive. This only means that you have a lot to worry about. As a team leader, there will be tough times in business, and you must steer your ship steady through it all. The business world is so dynamic that every few years, there are radical changes that ripple across the management sphere. Things change so fast, and you must make sure your team adapts equally as quickly. With the changes comes the demand for new roles, specialization, the division of labor and, in some cases, multitasking. You will learn useful techniques in neuro-linguistic programming that can help you identify strengths and weaknesses of your team members, and encourage them to take on new challenges.

Beating the competition

It is not easy staying ahead of the competition in the business world today. It only takes a few weeks before your competitors are neck-to-neck with you in terms of your unique selling point. At the moment, most companies resort to price wars, because they are virtually offering the same thing. Economic experts would advise, however, that price wars are a temporary solution. They never last. Over time, the hype created by price wars fizzles out, and consumers start asking the hard questions about utility and value proposition.

Managers need to learn how to survive and compete favorably in such markets. Instead of coming up with a panicky, reactive, and more often knee-jerk reaction to a competitor's proposition, you need to find a way to incorporate the entire workforce in coming up with a solution that is carefully thought through.

Besides, employee turnover is very high at the moment, because employees realize their worth. Instead of laboring in a dead-end job with very little prospect for growth, they move on to companies that are properly managed, that have a good vision and a visionary leadership structure. It is all about career growth and development, and as a manager, you can use neuro-linguistic programming to learn how to handle such scenarios at work.

Leadership vs. Ruling

It is amazing how many people confuse leadership and ruling. A leader should inspire people to achieve greater things. This is different from a ruler. A ruler simply gives instructions, or barks commands. A leader becomes a part of the team. They are involved in the daily activities that take place in the team, and the team feels closer to a leader than a ruler.

Proactive companies in this business environment have managed to thrive and survive tough times because they are careful in their recruitment of managers. They go for leaders, people who can lead their teams into a new future. Companies seek managers who forge strong relationships amongst their team members and foster a cohesive work environment.

Motivation is a key element of leadership. You have to motivate your team to work towards your vision for the company. On your part, you must also understand the individual goals and objectives that each person has, and align that with the roles you assign them, so that in the long run, they feel accomplished, and appreciate the work that they do for the team.

Management is about motivation rather than coercion. You need to understand this and make sure your employees also understand the same. It is like respect – it is a two-way street. For you to command respect, you have to give it to earn it.

Do not confuse fear with respect, as most people do. Employees who fear you will hardly ever respect you. They will shift camp at the earliest opportunity, and will never have your back when things get difficult.

You need people working with you, not working for you. You need employees who are willing to go the extra mile for you, so in return, you also should show them you are ready to do the same for them. This creates a sense of trust and loyalty, and before you know it, you will have a close-knit team working together. This, amongst other things, is what leadership is about, and is what sets your management style apart from a ruler.

Workforce morale

Everyone goes through a low moment in their life. At work, this happens all the time. Someone might have come to work against the backdrop of some challenges at home. Clearly, this is an individual who is not going to have a good day at work. Managers struggle to create or maintain good morale at work because some of them barely are able to understand or read the moods of their employees.

You cannot force things down on people. Even though you are a manager, you must realize that you are a human being first, and a manager second. The element of apathy should not dissipate into oblivion by virtue of the fact that you are a manager.

Work environments tend to struggle with different issues all the time, affecting the team morale in the process. Even in a disruptive environment, you need to be able to read people's minds and know when things are not okay. Each team has high and average performers. In a disruptive environment, a high performer can suffer when their mind is not in the right place. Your role is to try to get them back on track.

Procedure

There are things that you will learn from neuro-linguistic programming that will help you engage better with your employees, and give them the confidence they need to perform better. These include the following:

- Make sure your team understands what is expected of them in their current roles and positions.

- If someone performs well or does something out of the ordinary, ensure they receive the support and recognition of the team.

- Show genuine interest in your team. Do this in a way that the team members can feel assured of your genuine concern.

- If there is an opportunity for growth for any of the team members, make sure you let them know, and support them through it.

- People like to be listened to. Ensure you listen to your employees. Pay attention to the concerns they raise.

- You must make sure the team is motivated. Structure your teams in such a way that people can support one another and pull those who are lagging behind.

- One of the biggest concerns that most employees have with management is that you expect so much of them, but at the same time provide very little resources to work with. Make sure you provide the necessary resources to support your employees, and you will be happy with the turnout.

- Matching roles and responsibilities to abilities is important. You want people working on things that they are good at. This will save time, and help you keep the team motivated.

Talent and management go hand in hand. Talented employees who serve under poor managers eventually feel disengaged from the work and the company and move on to another company. It is not just the loss of the employee that you have to think about, but also the cost of replacing them. Recruitment, training, and induction are a costly affair for any company, and you should strive to avoid it by all means. The relationship between talented employees and their immediate supervisors makes a big difference and determines whether they will keep performing at their peak or not.

Passion in leadership

How badly do you want success in your field as a leader or a manager? Think about this analogy for a minute – how many superstar players have you seen coming back to become successful coaches? Very few of them do. What makes the difference between these players and their coaches? A player can be so good at what they do. They are perfect in the team and when working together with other players, they can achieve great things. However, this does not make the player a leader, a mentor, or a head coach. This is the same mentality that happens at work too.

Employees who have the best skills at certain tasks will not always make the best managers, because they might not know how to manage people. To be an effective manager, there are many skill sets that you should learn. Some people are natural leaders, while others learn how to lead.

As a leader, you must be passionate about the work you are doing and share the same passion with your team. This is one thing that will make them more motivated to work hard for you so that together, you can achieve the organizational goals and objectives. It is through your passion that you can also motivate them to go the extra mile for you.

You must show your team that what they are doing is important to you, and they mean a lot to you too. When you value your people highly, they appreciate it and strive to reciprocate it through their work. Passion is about meaningfulness. If people find something meaningful, it is easier to inspire passion in them.

Effective communication

You might be one of the most talented people in the office, but if you are unable to explain to your staff what they need to do in the best way possible, you will struggle to rally the troops. Most highly efficient teams communicate well with one another. Communication lines should be open so that your team can always reach you whenever they need something. You are more than just a leader, you are a mentor. You need to create that rapport with them so that they do not feel you are out of touch with what they are working on.

Chapter 8: Effective Listening Techniques

We live in a world that is full of distortions and distractions at every juncture. Faced with these challenges, a lot of people hear but barely listen. These are traits that have been responsible for many failed relationships, contracts, and many other engagements. Effective listening is a part of effective communication. If you listen to what someone is telling you, you create a rapport with them. You understand them and can respond to their needs better.

Business people understand the importance of effective listening, especially those in the sales departments. Competition is so stiff that you cannot afford to take any of your customers for granted. Effective listening is an important technique in neuro-linguistic programming that you need to learn if you are not doing it already. It can change your life and your prospects in whichever part of your life you feel you are falling short of expectations.

Through effective listening, you can get a deeper, better insight into the life of your customers, and other people around you. When you listen to what someone is saying, you see why they need your product, and understand how you can pitch it to their needs, not their ears.

The following are some useful neuro-linguistic programming techniques that can help you make the changes you need in your life, and improve your relations with those around you:

Understand your audience

Communication is as much about understanding your audience as it is about the message you are sharing with them. You need to first determine how they respond to messages, and how they interpret them. Your audience will either be a kinesthetic, auditory, \`or visual person. This is good information that can help you determine how to appeal to them.

If you are addressing customers, such information will help you know what appeals to them, and you can use this to determine their preferred purchase patterns. For visual customers, you need to use pictures in your presentation to get their attention. If you are dealing with an auditory customer, your sales pitch needs to make the most use of sound, and for kinesthetic customers, allow them the chance to interact with your products closely. Let them touch the products, feel the experience. These are useful neuro-linguistic programming approaches that will go a long way in helping you make progress not just in sales, but in many aspects of your life.

Active Listening

Everyone seems to be rushing somewhere these days. It is so difficult to find someone who will take time and listen to what you are talking about. Conversations end up being a competition, who will finish first?

Listening to people you are talking to helps you establish rapport with them. You need to make them feel you are not just wasting yours and their time, but you are serious about what you are talking about. You appreciate them, as much as you want them to appreciate the content you are sharing with them. Listening is also a good way of strengthening a relationship. How many times have you heard about people in relationships fighting because one party never seems to listen to the other?

Listening is not just about what you hear, it is also about what you see. There are non-verbal cues that are shared in communication, and you must learn to decode them. More often, these cues convey a lot more information than what is spoken.

Before you start a conversation with someone, consider their situation. Do you think they are feeling comfortable where they are? Are they nervous? Are you making them feel uncomfortable? How about yourself, are you comfortable? Are you nervous? Just in the same way you need to understand your audience, they also need to understand you. There are people in your audience who might have gone through neuro-linguistic programming training before, and they can read your mind based on what they see. If you are not presenting yourself as someone who is enjoying what they are doing, who is in control, why would they take you seriously?

Active listening is a give and take situation. You can only receive as much as you are willing to offer. Be enthusiastic about your message, and the enthusiasm will rub off on your audience, and they will reciprocate it. Consider the tone of your voice, your gestures, posture, and so forth. These are things that increase the chances that people will not just understand you, but they will be interested in learning more from you.

Careful choice of words

One of the lessons you learn in neuro-linguistic

programming is to choose the words you use carefully. This is a neuro-linguistic programming technique that has borne good results for so many people. There are different words that you can use in different situations. These are words that elicit certain responses. They are trigger words.

You use such words to induce the audience into a response. They might not know it yet, but you do. For example, words like change, happy, success, and believe are effective in creating a positive reaction. Using words like secret, truth, imagine, or expose create an element of curiosity in your audience. Do not just leave it at that; you can also emphasize certain words to drive your message home. Experts recommend repeating important phrases to turn them into commands.

Verbal cues are important because they create an avenue for a productive back and forth interaction. When speaking to someone, reflect their feelings and thoughts in the words you use. Try to emphasize the words that they speak to you by repeating them back in an assuring way. This gets them excited, and willing to carry the conversation further.

If someone in your audience does something, acknowledge it. Acknowledgment is about self-esteem and is one of the best ways for you to keep a positive line of communication while at the same time showing that you understand and listen to them. If you acknowledge someone, do it sincerely, and mean it.

Non-verbal cues

Appropriate body language can speak volumes. It can also show what you are feeling, and to your audience, show them that you are listening to what they are talking about. Non-verbal cues are useful in reinforcing a message, but at the same time, they can also come in handy when you are struggling with verbal communication.

Making eye contact is one of the best ways of showing someone that you are listening to them.

The secret is to make eye contact without appearing to be staring at someone. Assuming you are in a situation where you are taking notes, do not focus all your attention on the notes. Try to look up and make eye contact with the other party. Depending on the kind of interaction that you are having, some people might feel offended when you take notes. They need your undivided attention, and you should give it.

Are you frowning? Frowns will kill any conversation so fast. Try to smile a bit. Learn to smile. If you are making a presentation, spare time to learn a few facial expressions that can help you. Smiling or showing any sign of empathy is a natural way for you to show your audience that you are listening. While at it, try to avoid expressions that might show resentment, like shaking your head or raising your eyebrows. On the other hand, you can nod your head slightly in agreement with your audience, showing them that you have understood what they are talking about.

Study your posture. Try to lean slightly towards your audience, and keep an open posture. An open posture is a sign that you are willing to learn and are creating an engaging environment. However, even while you do that, try to make sure you do not lean so much that it feels you are invading someone's personal space.

These neuro-linguistic programming techniques are useful. However, it is also possible to overuse them. Overusing these techniques can also see your strategies fail terribly. To use them well, you must be authentic and sincere in your deeds. The neuro-linguistic programming techniques should come in as a booster to what you are doing and can improve your interactions with your audience.

Positivity

A positive conversational thought process will get you going places. People do not respond well to negativity. If you are searching for success, you must approach it with a positive mindset.

Positivity will also help to channel motivation from your audience and reprogram your mind towards achieving the targets you set out to.

Positivity is a part of reframing, one of the popular neuro-linguistic programming techniques. If, for example, you have not been having a very good time with sales, you probably feel downtrodden about it, and negative. Do not let this override the fact that you can change things for the better. It is all in your perspective. If you keep thinking about things from a failed point of view, you will keep failing. However, you can turn things around. Simple things like tastes, smells, or sounds can lift your moods, getting you in the perfect mood to make a good pitch.

Chapter 9: Managing Stress Through Neuro-Linguistic Programming

Stress and anxiety affect a lot of people. More often, stress is a product of the environment you are in. Stress can turn you into a slave for your emotions, and at times, someone else's emotions if you are unable to control it. Stress is a part of life, however. The body is built in such a way that it can handle stress. However, when the balance gets disrupted, you will suffer and it can affect your life negatively.

There are many challenges that you experience when you are unable to manage stress properly. You will live an unhealthy life, for a start. Individuals who are stressed most of the time suffer endocrine abnormalities and metabolic syndromes. These two are responsible for hypertension and obesity. You are at a higher risk of developing heart disease at this juncture. Reducing your stress level is important, as it will help your body get an immune boost, and at the same time reduce your chances of suffering allergic reactions, or even cancer.

Stress has a detrimental effect on relationships. Relationships barely survive given the challenges that exist in the normal environment. From work to pressure from society, relationships have to endure so much if they are to succeed. Introducing stress into the mix takes away energy that could have been used to build and nurture the relationship. Since you are always stressed, the people around you will also have to learn to choose their words carefully around you and be careful about what they do. This becomes an unpleasant situation, and before long, you set yourself apart from those around you.

One of the reasons why most people are unable to manage their tasks and schedules on time is because of stress. When you are stressed, you will barely meet your goals because your brain is distracted.

These are just a few of the challenges that you experience when you are struggling to manage stress in your life. Stress affects the quality of your life, and it is for this reason that you need to find a way of managing it effectively.

When unchecked, stress can bring devastation into your life. Unfortunately, it is almost impossible to avoid stress, given that you have to deal with financial problems, work concerns, and so many other things in your day to day endeavors. There are times when you might be stressed without being able to figure out the reason behind it. Stress can be a way for the body to communicate to you that it is struggling to adapt to certain changes in your immediate environment, a cry for help.

There are many ways you can manage stress. Meditation and deep breathing usually work for a lot of people. These are procedures that coupled with neuro-linguistic programming techniques, can help you learn how to manage stress and live a normal, productive life.

Is stress a bad thing? Of course, it is. This is almost the first thing anyone will tell you. However, since we are looking at neuro-linguistic programming, whose premise is behavior, belief, and attitude change, it is wise to let you know that you have thought about stress all wrong for most of your life. While stress has been admonished, it is not a bad thing. You could use some stress in your life to succeed. Here are some reasons why stress could be a good thing in your life:

- ***Completing tasks***

Stress can help you power through and complete important projects on time. Anyone who works in a busy environment will tell you this. You cannot have an easy attitude with projects. Some gigs put you under a lot of pressure, especially if you look at the time allocated for them or the specificity of the deliverables. If you do not stress over things like these, you will barely achieve anything in your career.

- ***Goal setting***

How do you go about your days, weeks, or months? Do you have goals? Or do you just work on the first thing that comes to mind when you wake up? Goal setting is one of those things that will cause you stress. However, it is a good kind of stress. Setting goals gives you something to work towards, an impetus to become a better person. You challenge things that stand in your way, look for possibilities, and reach out to people for collaboration, just so you can meet your goals, personal or otherwise. Isn't that some good stress?

- ***Managing change***

People generally do not like change. However, change is inevitable in this life. When something changes in your life, you must respond to it, and change accordingly too. The body will respond to changes in your life by inducing stress. Stress is its way of alerting you that something has changed, and you need to do something about it.

Stress is like an alarm for your body. If you understand how important your alarm is to waking you up on time and getting you ready for work, then you can look at stress in the same manner, and appreciate the changes it makes you perform to your body, and your environment.

- *__Motivation__*

Stress can be a good motivator. If you have something to work towards, you push your limits to make sure you achieve it. The idea lingers at the back of your mind so much until you get what you want. Most people who are working on or towards something big never stop thinking about it until they are done. Once you achieve what you want, the next step is to go further, to pursue greatness.

Neuro-linguistic programming for stress management

The premise of neuro-linguistic programming is that your subconscious creates perceptions of the situations you are going through based on the words that you use. This concept is deeply a part of meditation, especially when using positive affirmations. Everyone takes a different perspective on the things in their environment depending on the perception that they have. This further determines the realities in your life. It is from past experiences and perceptions that we are who we are at the moment, and these interactions determine the programming of the brain in the present moment.

While people might share the same backgrounds, their experiences prior to their present moment determine how they relate to situations around them. Body language and verbal communication are key to understanding why people do some of the things that they do. Through neuro-linguistic programming, you will learn a number of techniques that can be useful in managing stress and can also help you in self-development and progress.

Neuro-linguistic programming is about the

organization of thoughts in your head. If you are keen, you will realize that when you are under a lot of stress, you barely think straight. Everyone has unique filters which allow them to see the world in different ways, depending on their circumstances, and the experiences that they might have had in the past.

Managing stress depends on how your mind processes information. People who process information visually will always create images in their minds whenever they need to respond to a question. People who process information kinesthetically have a predisposition to emotional appeal when responding to things in their environment. Those who respond to auditory messages respond to sounds to address issues.

By understanding these three categories, it is easy to create a good starting point for stress management. There are many tools that can assist you in managing stress and reducing the symptoms. Take note that neuro-linguistic programming should not be misconstrued as a magical system. Even with the tools and techniques that you will learn, you must still strive to live a constructive and productive life.

There are three basic techniques that you can learn, which will help you with stress management. These techniques are also recommended for anxiety relief:

- Reframing
- Sub-modality alteration
- Relaxation anchoring (trance)

Reframing

When you are stressed, you have a unique view of the world and things that go on around you. Changing this perception will go a long way in helping you manage the situation better. If you take a deeper look at stress, it is not always a bad thing. There are situations where stress can spur you to work harder and achieve greater things. Most people see stress as a negative feeling.

If you take a positive approach to life, stress can be a motivational factor. It keeps you thinking about something, your goals, and planning ways of getting there. Think about it for a moment. If stress did not exist, would you have any challenges in life? Without challenges, life would be plain and boring. You would live in a perpetual comfort zone, unaware of the possibility of scaling new heights, or discovering new things that could make your life better.

In neuro-linguistic programming, therefore, you learn how to change the negative view you have of stress, and look at it from a positive point of view. When you do this, you can turn something that would normally harm you and make your life difficult into a stepping stone for a satisfying life. The good thing about the body is that it is built ready for such changes. The human body was engineered for survival. You are always looking for something to solve. At the same time, the brain keeps looking for ways of keeping you safe. In an attempt to keep you safe, your brain tries to mitigate dangerous situations, make you aware and keep you safe. While this is a good thing, it is also the same thing that might be holding you back.

Unknown to most people, fear can keep you safe. Since you are afraid of something, you look for ways of protecting yourself. How can you learn to reframe stress so that you see things differently? First, whenever you are feeling stressed, know that something has changed in your life or your immediate environment, and you have to address it. Once you recognize this, you can then reframe the situation in your mind, and learn to alter your behavior.

Reframing introduces the prospect of a primary positive result and a secondary benefit that you can derive from any of your behavior patterns. Ideally, when you are reframing, you are in a negotiation with your subconscious mind to figure out what you can benefit from the situation at hand. Away from your subconscious, stress is a way for the body to communicate with your consciousness, telling you that something is not right, or something has changed. You just need to figure out what it is, and how to address it.

Looking at stress in this manner can change your life. The secondary benefit that we mentioned is an opportunity cost of not dealing with the issue at hand. You can actually benefit from not overcoming the problem that is stressing you up. What we learn here is that each behavior has a payoff. Unfortunately, the secondary benefits are barely conscious. A good example is turning down a good job offer, perhaps because you are used to the sympathy you get when people tell you how stressful your current job is. If you were to take the new job, chances are high that you would enjoy it, and you would not have much to complain about. At the same time, you would no longer receive sympathy.

In neuro-linguistic programming, learning how to reframe a situation can help you manage stress properly because you will learn how to react differently to it, and this makes a big difference.

Sub-modality alteration

Another way of managing stress through neuro-linguistic programming is by altering the sub-modalities. Sub-modalities help you to change the impact that specific memories have in your life. By altering sub-modalities, you can either weaken bad memories so that they no longer have a very strong hold on you or strengthen good memories to cheer you up.

For someone whose life has a predisposition for stress, altering sub-modalities is a very useful neuro-linguistic programming technique that you should learn. Away from the difficulty in the name, this is one of the simplest neuro-linguistic programming techniques to manage stress. Altering sub-modalities refer to changing individual components of a given situation or memory. You can focus on the distance between the object and yourself, the colors, the sounds, anything that your mind can recall.

Once you settle on the item, you can change it to

suit whichever purpose you prefer. For good memories, you can learn to make them brighter and powerful, so that you feel better whenever you think about them. In the case of a bad memory or situation, you learn to push it further away, weakening their hold on your mind in the process, and helps you feel much better. For stress management, altering sub-modalities is one of the easiest neuro-linguistic programming techniques you will ever learn.

Relaxation anchoring (Trance)

Anchoring is another simple technique, because all you have to do when you are stressed is to close your eyes and think about a situation or something that happened in your life that comforts you. It should be a relaxing experience. With your eyes closed, you can also incorporate some meditation techniques like taking a deep breath, holding your breath in, and so forth. Another way is to create a visually appealing situation, like thinking of a time you went to the beach, and how awesome it was.

Anchoring is not just about thinking about the good moments. You must get yourself comfortable enough to the point where you feel you are physically in the moment. If your happy place is a walk by the beach, you should stay in the moment long enough for you to feel the sand under your feet or the warmth of the sun on your back. Can you feel the waves of the sea? The wind as the waves splash against the rocks? When you get into this state, stay here as long as you feel comfortable. This will help you let go of the stressful thoughts and focus on something that calms you down. Stay calm as long as you want to.

To establish the anchor, you can touch your index finger and thumb. While in the moment of tranquility, you can also think about a positive moment, creating a fist while at it. The more frequently you do this, the easier it will be for this moment to stick. Whenever you are feeling stressed, you can go back to this moment as your anchor and think about the positive sentiments.

Learning these simple neuro-linguistic programming techniques can make a big difference in your life. You will no longer see stress as a bad thing, but take the negativity around it, and turn it into a positive thing. After all, neuro-linguistic programming is all about changing behaviors and attitudes. A positive attitude towards stress is something very few people have. Try it today and see how it will change your life.

Chapter 10: Creating an Enabling and Motivational Environment for Teamwork

Managing the workforce is not an easy task. A lot of managers can admit to that. You need to create an enabling environment for your teams and go the extra mile to keep them motivated enough to keep working for the team. There is a concept in human resource that discredits money as a source of motivation at work. What this means is that you need to look towards non-monetary ways of keeping the team motivated and maintaining an enabling work environment.

There are different ways of motivating employees. Most of the factors that motivate employees will only work for a given period of time. Monetary gains might work for some employees, but this never lasts. What you need to do is create an enabling environment where the employees feel comfortable working for the team. This is one of the biggest motivators that is often overlooked by a lot of managers.

A motivated employee has a higher impetus to carry out their tasks better and meet their responsibilities. Within the first six months after someone is hired, the excitement fizzles out, as they get used to the routine. This gets worse for people whose roles are mundane. After a while, they start toying with the idea of a career shift or looking for a job elsewhere.

Reasons for Demotivation

A good part of the global workforce do not like their jobs. Most people feel their work contributes to a majority of their stress signals. For team leaders, managers, and anyone else in a position of power, these are dire statistics. With a majority of the workplace dissatisfied with their work opportunities, the prospect of a high employee turnover is very high. Employee turnover further means that the company has to spend more on recruitment, orientation, and induction.

What really causes this level of disenfranchisement, and how can neuro-linguistic programming help team leaders turn things around? The following are some of the main reasons that are fronted for dissatisfaction in the workplace:

- ***Uncertainty***

As a team manager, you will have to deal with conflict from time to time. You have individuals who excel when they work independently, and others who can only thrive in a team. Cooperation as a team means sharing responsibilities. This might not be easy on everyone, especially for people who are yet to work with teams in their employment history.

The fact that the employee has to work with other people can create an element of confusion in terms of their role within the team. More often you end up with duplicity of tasks when different members are working on the same thing. You might also end up not having the core tasks handled. These are some of the challenges that you must be ready to address as the team manager.

- ***Poor Management***

At the helm of the list of reasons that people give for dissatisfaction at work, poor management takes the crown. A lot of companies employ micromanagement for different reasons. However, when micromanagement is not done properly, it ends up creating a situation worse than what it was intended to solve.

One of the risks of micromanagement is that it takes away the life from the workforce. Most micromanagers, even if they mean well, end up turning into overlords, creating apathy in the workplace. Most employees see micromanagement as an inference that they do not know what they are doing and must be constantly supervised. If the company does not trust an employee to do their work without supervision, they soon feel like their input is not valued, and start looking for a way out.

- ***Insecurity***

Job security is a problem all over the world. You can go home from work one day and come back in the morning to realize you are jobless. Companies have shut down overnight, and this is not just something you see in the movies – *it is real!*

If the company is not doing well, the instability seeps down to the employees. The most they can do is invest in the company to the extent of their paychecks. Most of the time, such employees will always be looking for something else. This is a team that will spend a lot of time on rumors and gossip, looking busy on their computer screens when in the real sense they are polishing their resumes and orchestrating their next move should your ship sink.

When you are facing turbulent times, it becomes difficult for any leader to hold on to some of the best talents they have. The only way you can combat this is to engage them frequently, communicate with them directly and truthfully so that they can learn to trust you and stay loyal. It is impossible to coerce people into staying put, but by encouraging a line of transparency, it is easier to mitigate some of the surprise moves.

- ***Lack of Progress***

People need to feel the work they are doing matters to someone. You need to belong to something. If the company is making a big move and you were part of the planning process, you need to associate with the final outcome.

Companies that are struggling to get their act together barely have any room for progress. There is too much red tape around, making it difficult for employees to make the next step in their career. At an entry level, most employees are excited about their salaries. However, a few years into the job, salaries do not mean much if there is no room for growth and development.

- ***Leadership Integrity***

The kind of leadership that exists in the company is often responsible for the feeling of disenfranchisement that sweeps across the company. Employees will not always love all the leaders, but they need to see and believe that the leadership is capable of steering the company in the right direction. Without this, loyalties shift so fast, and people will be looking to either ditch the camp, or stay but become subversive. There are very few leaders in the workplace who can inspire change and confidence, communicating with their employees in a way that inspires their vision.

- ***Poor Communication***

Poor communication or lack thereof is another reason why employees struggle to stay or feel motivated in the workforce. Without information, you create an opportunity for conspiracy theories and rumors. People work through guesses, confusion, and frustration. You end up spending a lot of time searching for information to clarify certain positions, instead of doing your job.

- ***Unfruitful Partnerships***

The composition of the teams at work play an important role in employee satisfaction and motivation. Many are those who are in jobs that are not necessarily paying well, but they are surrounded by people who make them feel like they are part of a family, a well-knit team that goes out of its way to work together and enjoy life outside their work dynamics.

A strong team cohesion is not something that you can overstate. If you are in a position that earns you a lot of money but there is no rapport with your teammates, you will feel empty and, before you know it, you will have to keep watching your back to save yourself from misery, stress, and backstabbing. While it is not necessary that you end up with best friends at work, you should work in an environment that allows you to feel relaxed around the people you work with, and at least enjoy the pleasure of working together.

Role of neuro-linguistic programming in the workplace

In your capacity as a team leader, manager, or in whichever position of authority, your task is to make sure you can create an environment that not only motivates employees to work but keeps their enthusiasm alive.

You should include neuro-linguistic programming skills in your leadership to improve your influence and capacity to coach, communicate, and motivate the team you work with. Through neuro-linguistic programming, you learn changes that can help you become flexible and improve the motivation and performance of your team.

Through neuro-linguistic programming, you should be able to interact with your team members in such a way that you get them to do what you want, but through a constructive approach. Neuro-linguistic programming considers the diversity that exists in the workplace. Everyone cannot share the same perspective all the time. The following are some of the simple ways neuro-linguistic programming can help you manage and motivate the team:

- ***Managing Workplace Stress***

Stress is a normal part of the average modern workforce. The sources of stress are either external or internal. Things like poor resource management can stress you and your team out. You are in no position to control all the stress factors. However, what you can do is manage how you respond or react to them. Learn to interpret stress signals positively and you will be able to change your thought process and that of your team. This allows you to reprogram your minds, and learn how to overcome and conquer the stressors.

- ***Right of Way***

Success is determined by how you communicate

with people around you. A team manager always needs to make sure they get the team performing according to the set terms and conditions, or the objectives at hand. With this in mind, your success will depend on the presentations and requests, and how well you communicate them to your team. The team has to understand what you require of them, or they will fall short of expectations. When discussing prospects with your team members, you have to consider the sentiments that motivate them to be where they are.

- ***Handling Processes***

Through your communique, you must establish the difference between processes and content, and the role that each member has to play in either. You have to be keen on the conversations that go on during group meetings. Monitor the tones, gestures, and any other non-verbal cues from your team. These cues provide the best way for you to determine the real problem that the individuals are trying to put across. Based on this assessment, you can then find an amicable way to structure the content you share in the meeting so that you can avert a crisis in the case of tension, or where necessary, push a specific discussion forward to a later meeting.

- *Establishing Cooperative Independence*

One of the things you have to do as a team manager is to ensure that everyone in your team understands their style, and can adapt to your mode of communication. You are working towards creating an accommodating environment for the team, so communication is an important part of this. Even though you are creating a team, you must also realize that there are people who might be more comfortable and efficient when they work independently, while there are those who thrive in a group scenario.

Your role would be to understand the needs of each team member and make sure that you find a way to align them with the overall team goals.

Finding the right balance between independence and cooperation is not always an easy thing to do, but when you get it right, your team will benefit from a conducive business environment.

Departmental benefits of neuro-linguistic programming

In any progressive workforce, neuro-linguistic programming lies at the center of convictions and techniques that spur personal growth. Managers are put through neuro-linguistic programming techniques during training sessions so that they can learn how to best interact with their employees and their peers.

Neuro-linguistic programming can be used to influence motivation and cooperation between employees, in the process improving the nature of communication with stakeholders like clients. One of the best things about neuro-linguistic programming is that you stand to gain a lot from it, whether at a personal or professional level. Here are some of the benefits that different departments can gain from neuro-linguistic programming:

- ***Healthcare***

Patients and doctors must establish a rapport if they are to communicate effectively. Whether this is in the hospital or the workplace dispensary, creating a line of communication requires trust and confidence. Through neuro-linguistic programming, it is possible to establish positive contact between both parties and in the right way.

- ***Sales***

Communication skills are important to sales teams. This is the only way they can interact with clients and increase the leads. The customers need to be excited about the prospect of purchasing from you, and you can only do this by creating an environment where the customer trusts you and can ask you questions about the product or service, even if they are intimate questions.

- ***Education***

In the education sector, neuro-linguistic programming helps in improving the learning activities of students. Since education never ends at school, even in the workplace, you will benefit from learning certain neuro-linguistic programming techniques. This makes it easier for you to grasp new knowledge, learn skills that can help you adapt to work faster, and feel motivated to keep performing and meeting your targets.

- ***Welfare Service***

Counselors and therapists have unique ways of reaching out to their patients. Other than the treatment methods that they use, you can also benefit from learning some neuro-linguistic programming techniques to empower the process of psychotherapy. The good thing is that these experts can use neuro-linguistic programming either on its own as a form of treatment, or together with some other tried and tested treatment techniques to manage things like depression, stage fright, addiction, and anxiety.

- ***Management***

At the management level, neuro-linguistic programming skills are useful when it comes to coaching a team. These skills will help you learn how to handle conflicts, motivate your team, and more importantly, learn how to self-manage.

Improving teamwork through neuro-linguistic programming

Teamwork requires effort from the team members and the team manager. Through the neuro-linguistic programming techniques, you learn how to create an enabling environment where your team members are motivated and encouraged to work for the greater goals of the team. Teamwork is also about integrity and fostering a unified front while working towards becoming an important part of the workplace culture. The following are some of the things that you can do to create an enabling environment at work, having mastered the relevant neuro-linguistic programming techniques:

- ***Asking for help***

There is nothing wrong with asking for help. It is not a sign of weakness either. Asking for help is an important part of teamwork. You draw upon the strengths of individual members to uplift one another and eventually uplift the entire team. This support is useful especially when you need inspiration to go the extra mile.

- ***Division of labor***

Specialization and division of labor are key to effective teamwork. Everyone cannot do everything at the same time. For organization, you must break down tasks into small, manageable bits so that each party has something they are working on. Division of labor further helps you identify unique strengths that each member has, respective to the task they have been assigned, and you can build upon that for future reference.

- ***Speaking up***

Working together as a team means you have to communicate often as you work towards the goal. The team must be in contact with one another. Note down the milestones that should be achieved, and create an avenue where team members provide updates on their progress.

- ***Evaluation and review***

Reviews are an important part of any project because they help you get a glimpse of the project from someone else's eyes. Through the evaluation process, you open a platform where members can criticize the work that has been done, and raise questions where applicable. This makes it easier to address issues that would have otherwise been missed.

- ***Winning together***

Having struggled together as a team, you should celebrate the wins together, however small they might be. Spare time away from the project or from work to celebrate the contributions that each member brings to the team. These celebrations bring the team closer and strengthen the bond they share.

Neuro-linguistic programming provides skills and techniques that are useful in building and managing a strong and motivated team. By creating an enabling environment for the team, it becomes easier for each of the team members to learn and improve their personal skills too.

In neuro-linguistic programming, one of the most important lessons that you learn is the need to own a problem instead of blaming it on someone else. Blames are common in teams, but they often create chaos and fallouts. Even if each member approaches the task from a different perspective or style, your team should be able to appreciate the contribution and approach of one another. You need to get your team working together as a unit in order to achieve your targets. Focus on the bigger picture. Dwelling on failures will only make the decline progress further. Where one member falls short, the team can supplement with the strengths of another member. That is how neuro-linguistic programming works.

Chapter 11: Establishing Quality Relationships

Communication is a contentious issue in many relationships. We have come across or been in relationships that fell apart because the participants were unable to communicate properly. It does not matter the effort you put into a relationship, if you are unable to communicate effectively, all this will be futile.

Communication challenges are rife in relationships, especially in this age and time when there is a lot of technological distortion. Many relationships struggle because people are focusing their attention on things that do not matter. We struggle to forge relationships with people and things outside the relationship, to the point where we start losing the connection. A quick sample of some of the reasons why couples usually end up in therapy to save their relationships reveals a lack of communication as one of the common reasons.

Relationships do not necessarily have to be romantic relations. In the context of neuro-linguistic programming, relationships could also refer to any interaction you have with someone on a regular basis, whether at work or at home or in school. You form a unique bond or relationship with the people you interact with on a regular basis.

How does communication become a problem?

- *Language concerns*

Over time, we get used to certain sentiments or actions, to the point where we take them for granted. This is the point where communication starts breaking down, and a relationship that was once fulfilling becomes mundane. Poor communication wrecks the core of the relationship, shaking its foundation.

The language that is used in a relationship evolves to become a problem. A quality relationship is one where teamwork and partnership are at the helm of all activities. Whatever happens, you are always comfortable in the fact that someone has your back. Relationships are about us, not *I*.

As time goes, the language changes from a consultative perspective to a directive-based language. You realize that most of the communication revolves around *you*, or *I*. The concern that arises here is that such statements are often used to pass judgement, give directions or to order someone. It is belittling, and the longer communication is done in this manner, the more the relationship loses value.

Most people do not like to be told what to do. The assumption for any mature relationship is that there are two adults who know what is required of them, present in the relationship at all times. As an adult, if someone has to keep telling you what to do, this eventually affects your emotions. It feels like the person does not see you as an individual who can take charge, who can act on a cause without supervision

At this juncture, communication turns into defensiveness and resentment. This becomes a problem because when one party feels they have had enough, *no* becomes the default response, which soon spirals into conflict and disagreement.

- ***Generalized assumption***

No one likes to have their character generalized. Generalization makes you feel like you belong to a herd. It takes away the specialty element in a relationship, and more often, generalizations are negative. A keen look at most of the generalization statements shows that they almost always are combined with *you*.

Some examples include:

You are doing it wrong again

Why are you always so lazy?

You always do this

Everyone knows you cannot do it

I knew it had to be you

The use of such general and universal statements creates many problems in any relationship. The person who speaks such generalizations automatically assumes that the recipient is unable to do anything, or be anything better than the generalization that has been created. This can be so disheartening, especially when generalizations keep coming from someone you hold in high regard or someone who should have your back.

Generalizations tend to focus more on what has been done wrong, than how to make something better. They focus on blame, instead of what next. Such generalizations will only make the blame feel worse, especially for someone who is already struggling with the fact that they have fallen short of expectations. In the long run, generalizations only succeed in discouraging the individual from initiating a process that would bring about positive change and progress.

Just as we mentioned above about language concerns, generalizations leave very little room for positive discourse and instead open an avenue for retorting and disputes. It is easier to respond to a generalization with a contradictory statement in an attempt to prove a point than it is to address the issue at hand amicably.

- ***Evasive communication***

Communication involves a behavior or issue that is being addressed and the person to whom it is addressed to. For effective communication, a communicator needs to understand how to separate the person from the issue. This is not always easy. Ideal communication requires that the communicator goes tough on the issue in question, and soft on the recipient. However, this rarely happens. A lot of people do the reverse, they are soft on the issue but tough on the recipient.

Such communication easily spirals into personal

conflict, in the process ignoring the issue that should have been addressed, and focusing more on pinning down someone with personal barbs at their supposed inefficiency.

Toughening up on the individual could evoke negative responses or reactions from them. People take your personal attacks on them to heart. They become resentful, afraid, hurt, resistant, angry, and all manner of negative responses to the situation. These interactions will also involve a lot of "*you* or *I*" statements, and by the end of it, the issue that was to be discussed will have been missed by miles. You end up creating a personal conflict where none existed or was necessary.

- ***Invalidation***

Nothing hurts more than invalidation of your feelings. Invalidation takes place when someone recognizes your emotions, whether they approve of them or not, and instead of responding to them or acknowledging them, they dispute, minimize, belittle, ignore, discount, or judge them negatively.

One of the challenges with invalidation is that today, most people struggle to open up and talk about what they feel. Most of the interactions that people have are but a façade. The real communication and interaction take place in the gestures and non-verbal expressions that people make, over what is verbally spoken.

Invalidating someone's feelings diminishes their appeal and their positivity. They see you differently. They become afraid to open up and speak their minds whenever they are around you because they already know what you think of them. At times someone opens up about something that is so dear to them, an issue that would have been a starting point towards their progress. Invalidating such opinions makes an individual retreat into their cocoon.

With the decline in positive vibes in a relationship, it follows that the strength of the relationship will also wither. Invalidating opinions and feelings soon manifest into lingering and intense negativity, and as the negativity grows, barriers to communication in a relationship soar higher.

Invalidation causes resentment on the part of the recipient. The party whose feelings are invalidated will feel angry and hurt. The trust that they have in you goes away. Some people even shut you out completely, so that they do not have to risk you hurting them. Many relationships have suffered invalidation, and it is also one of the reasons why people fall out in friendships, with their families or people that they share a common bond with.

In light of the language concerns, generalized assumptions, evasive communication, and invalidation, communication in any relationship will suffer. Soon, the relationship deteriorates, parties become defensive, and conflict becomes the new normal. Since staying in this situation becomes untenable, three options are readily available: flight, fight, or freeze.

Some people would choose to confront or fight a poor communicator, move away from any situation that involves the poor communicator, or freeze all communication. Whichever of these options you choose in the aftermath of poor communication, the communication barriers will have been erected. These barriers also hinder growth and development, and any relationship that might have been linked to the main relationship could also be affected by the fallout. Both the sender and recipient in this communication line eventually suffer.

The role of neuro-linguistic programming in creating quality relationships

An important aspect of quality communication is to establish rapport with the audience. Through neuro-linguistic programming, you can learn a reliable and easy way of improving your communication skills.

By establishing rapport with someone, you reduce the differences that exist between the two factions and emphasize the similarities. Rapport brings a sense of mutual acceptance, recognition, and harmony in communication because you feel at ease with each other. Rapport further helps to smoothen the lines of communication. If you are a keen communicator, you will realize that creating rapport with your audience is a natural process.

If you are unable to create a natural rapport, you can create it deliberately in order to foster a therapeutic relationship, through neuro-linguistic programming. This can be achieved in the following manner:

Mirroring and Matching

Mirroring and matching can be misconstrued to mean copying, but this is not the case. Copying would, in fact, disengage the rapport. Mirroring is about reflecting the non-verbal communication cues that your audience makes, back to them in such a manner that they feel comfortable around you, and the communication can proceed naturally.

In this process, you are supposed to maintain a subtle approach that establishes a comfortable and trusted line of communication with the other person, without interfering with their conscious awareness.

Physical Mirroring

Physical mirroring is about responding to non-verbal cues in a similar manner, making it seem like the patient is staring at themselves in a mirror. Physical mirroring can be tricky because if it is not done subtly, it might look like copying, which breaks the line of communication.

If, for example, you are talking to someone, you can mirror their volume, pace, pitch or tonal variation. Another option would be to mirror the hand gestures someone makes when they are talking to you.

Physical mirroring also progresses into **verbal mirroring**. In verbal mirroring, you use the same pitch, pace, tone, and voice that the individual is using. Another way of doing this would be to repeat the last words that they say in a sentence from time to time, but by adding a light question inflexion to them.

Kinesthetic Language

Kinesthetic language refers to the use of phrases and words that express a feeling. It is about using words to suggest a feeling or make the recipient think about how they feel about what has been said to them. Some simple examples include:

This does not feel right, does it?

This makes a lot of sense right now

How will this affect me?

I feel I need to understand this better before we can proceed

Kinesthetic language, when coupled with

auditory and visual language cues in the right manner, can make a big difference in the way communication takes place. Over time, you will learn the communication style that different people prefer, and with it, the language patterns that are suitable for the same.

Before you start learning the language patterns that are suitable for someone, it is important that you learn what works for you. It is by understanding who you are that you can open up to appreciating the differences between others and yourself, and learning how they communicate. Building on this, you will know what sensory channels are common in your language, and learn how to match these to your audience.

Important communication lessons from neuro-linguistic programming

Individuals who can create and sustain mutually productive, quality relationships with people around them usually enjoy more success than those who do not. For some people, establishing good relationships is like second nature. However, even if they are good at it, quality communication is a skill that has to be developed over time. Here are some important lessons that you will learn from neuro-linguistic programming regarding quality communication:

- ***Communication is mandatory***

There is never a time when communication stops. Communication is all around us. Whether you are speaking or not, there is some form of communication taking place. A couple that fights and stops talking to one another is communicating their frustration and anger at each other, or the situation they find themselves in.

Communication is not just about words, it involves a lot more, including gestures. What makes the difference in your relationships and interactions is your awareness of the fact that communication never ends, unconscious, non-verbal, or verbal. There are times when you communicate without knowing you are.

The first step towards establishing quality communication and relationships with others around you is to become aware of the fact that you are always communicating. Becoming aware of your environment, the sentiments, feelings, and attitudes toward you is a crucial step in communication because it awakens your consciousness on the interactions that take place around you.

- ***Yours isn't the only perspective***

Most people address reality from their perspective. Anything that challenges their view is wrong. This is not true. Through neuro-linguistic programming, we learn to understand our view of the world, through the filters, expectations, and values that we have built over the years. This is why we lock people out when they do things contrary to what we believe in.

Neuro-linguistic programming reminds you that

it is easier to understand how others behave around you by welcoming the idea that their model of the world as it is, is just as perfect as yours is. Everyone does not have to see the world through your eyes. At times, you need to see the world through theirs. This simple reality allows you to understand why people behave the way they do, and you embrace them for who they are.

- ***Response determines value in communication***

Communication is meaningless if it does not elicit any response. Therefore, response determines how important communication is. More often, it is easier to cast blame on someone because they do not understand your message. However, according to what you learn in neuro-linguistic programming, you are responsible for your messages. If you are unable to communicate the message effectively, you are unable to communicate at all.

What we learn from this is the need for flexibility.

For you to interact with people and share your knowledge, it is important that you learn to speak in a way that they understand you. Learn more about their experience, their perspective, and the environment. This gives you a better chance of communicating with them accordingly.

One of the biggest challenges that a lot of people have when communicating is that they always put their perspective first, ahead of everyone else. At times you have to embrace changes so that you can learn to communicate well with others around you. Take the example of a firm that barely interacts with people on social media, but social media is the main source of interaction for their target audience. This company will need to consider setting up social media accounts that are popular with their audience, and from there, learn more about the things that their audience respond to, and communicate with them on the same wavelength.

Communication is as much about the originator as it is about the message that is being shared. If you are unable to share your message, you need to rethink your method of delivery.

- ***Communication is a resource-based skill***

For you to develop positive and healthy relationships with people around you, you need to understand why they behave in the manner that they do. You need to look at things from their point of view. An example is given of a toddler whose only way of communication is to cry to get attention. The toddler cries because, at that point in life, that is the option available to them.

Each behavior is related to an intention. If you have to, consider making new resources available for your audience, and it might improve the mode and nature of communication. In the long run, creating new ways of communication can help you forge a stronger relationship with the people around you.

- ***You are in control***

One thing you learn about communication in neuro-linguistic programming is that you are always in control. You bear responsibility for the way you interact with people. Communication is a cause and effect scenario. You will either consider yourself in control of the situation and with the power to determine how the communication will manifest, or you can either put the blame on circumstances or someone to explain why you are not successful in communication.

In either of the scenarios, you are in control. In case the communication approach is not fruitful, you should think about how you can change your behavior to alter the course of the communication. In a causative position, your aim should be learning and understanding the recipient's point of view, so you can communicate in a way they understand.

- ***Separating people from behaviors***

Individuals are independent of their behaviors. In neuro-linguistic programming, the primary concept is that individuals often work with what they have at their disposal to deliver their best. If people had different or more tools of communication than what they have, the course of communication would be different than what you are looking at.

To foster healthy relationships with those around you, you need to learn not to judge someone according to their behavior. Behavior can be influenced by many things. As you grow, you learn and interact with different people, and these interactions shape your beliefs. If you take time to learn, you can easily turn the course of a bad relationship, and save yourselves from potential emotional ruin.

Everyone desires a relationship where they are cherished and feel complete, a partner that supports them and compliments them in whatever they do. Relationships should be special and fulfilling. They are about respect and values, and a commitment to the common goal. Though most people barely get all these, it is possible to get it all. You might have different reasons for being in the relationship with your partner. What is important is that you both look at yourselves from different perspectives and appreciate your differences.

Set and work on realistic goals that you can both achieve. Clear all the negativity you might have, emotional sentiments that might be holding you back, and work towards a new frontier. Identify any restricting beliefs that you might have about your relationship and push them out of the way. With neuro-linguistic programming, you have all the tools you need to rebuild your life and create an amazing relationship.

Chapter 12: Ethical Manipulation in Neuro-Linguistic Programming

Mind control is a term that invokes different thoughts from people. There are others who are immediately scared when you mention mind control, and rightly so. No one wants to be manipulated into doing things that they are unaware of. On the other hand, neuro-linguistic programming teachers mind control, but for a good reason. Mind control in neuro-linguistic programming is to help you make progress, change a bad situation into a good one.

The mind responds to perceptions better than anything else. What someone believes in their mind goes a long way. Mind control can be used to influence actions because it changes the thoughts which the mind had control over. There are specific patterns and strategies that are used in neuro-linguistic programming for mind control. The challenge in neuro-linguistic programming is to change someone's mind for the better, and not take advantage of them in the process.

Mind control is like hacking. We have ethical hackers and unethical hackers. Unethical hackers go about their trade for nefarious reasons. Ethical hackers, on the other hand, hack systems for a good reason. They try to identify and fix problems, and more often, your systems are safer after an ethical hacker has done their job. The same applies to mind control. There are some basic principles that guide mind control in neuro-linguistic programming, which support the cause for ethical manipulation.

Control over thoughts

The mind works in a very simple way, cause and effect. Experts can monitor brainwaves and understand what goes on in the mind through an EEG. This scan will show your consciousness, how alert you are, and the level of activity that takes place in your head. In a beta state, the brain experiences very high frequencies.

You experience a state of calm when the brain is in alpha state. Alpha state is characterized by low frequencies. In this state, your brain barely handles any thoughts. This is an important state of the mind as it induces calmness. It is also the state where hypnosis takes place, and experts can also induce subconscious mind programming.

In hypnosis, the expert will try to get your mind into the alpha state. While in this state, it is easier for your brain to receive commands which can then be programmed. Through neuro-linguistic programming, you learn techniques that can be used to induce thoughts that the individual will not notice consciously, into their unconscious mind.

Neuro-linguistic programming focuses on persuasion. This is a strategy whose persuasive approach is very strong and explains why it is often used in socializing, marketing, politics, and business.

Perceptions

Your thoughts are often influenced by your perception of the signals around an event. Based on this knowledge, it is possible to change your thought process by creating an obstacle or introducing a new subject which will be picked by the subconscious mind, and bypass the conscious mind. The subconscious mind can be influenced by very subtle suggestions. The mind is limited beyond perceptions. There are so many remarkable things that can be done to the mind through programming.

Techniques used in mind control

Each expert has their unique techniques that they can use for mind control. These techniques usually depend on the nature of the event or situation that is being addressed. Each individual is unique, as are the situations they deal with. The following are some of the techniques that experts use for mind control:

Focusing on the individual

An expert will pay attention to the client. They try to notice all cues, verbal or non-verbal. Non-verbal cues usually give the best hint of what an individual is going through. Experts will focus on things like body flush, dilation of the pupils, breathing patterns, and so forth. These cues can give so much information about the individual.

It is easy to read the mind of an individual because the non-verbal cues usually are aligned with their emotions. It is by studying these cues that the expert can determine how the individual processes and perceives the information that they come across.

A good example is when the individual is asked something like the color of their shoes, and while giving their answer, their eyes shift to the top right corner, then it is clear that their response is a visual creation. However, if the eyes shift to the top left corner, then theirs is a visual remembrance creation.

Suggestive frequency

The heart beats at between 45 and 72 beats per minute. To influence the mind, the expert can speak to the individual at a suggestive frequency within this range. This is the same frequency that the human mind operates at. In so doing, the mind is more suggestible.

Voice roll

Using a voice roll is a good way to bypass the conscious mind. A voice roll is a technique that involves a pattern style where the expert emphasizes a specific word that the individual relates to but in a monotonous pattern.

Anchoring

The expert creates an anchor for the patient. Once an anchor is programmed into the mind, all the expert needs to do is touch or tap on the patient to put them in a specific state. Anchors offer a sublime way of programming the mind.

Creating rapport

Creating rapport is the most basic form of mind control. Neuro-linguistic programming experts use this to create a sense of suggestibility. Rapport is created by examining the individual and their body language. Once the expert understands the body language, this can be used to make you vulnerable to the expert's suggestions.

Using specific words

Neuro-linguistic programming experts have specific words that they can use to trigger emotions or responses from the patient. Most of these words are patterned in such a way that they are permissive and suggestive, but most people would see them as normal words. These words are often linked to sensual suggestions and are effective in creating a mental picture that changes the perception of the mind. Apart from suggestive words, the expert can also use vague words which help them control your thought process.

Subconscious mind programming

Subconscious mind programming is done through an interspersal method. In neuro-linguistic programming, this involves the expert getting you to focus on one thing, and while your mind is focused on it, they insert a new idea or concept in your subconscious mind.

Chapter 13: Setting and Meeting Goals

At the turn of the year, a lot of people flood social media with goals they are aiming to achieve over the coming weeks. Not so many people meet these goals, unfortunately. The reason for this is because most of the goals do not have any basis, nor is there a guideline on how to achieve them. Just saying you are out to do one or two things is not going to get you there.

The basic principle behind goal setting is that your targets are supposed to be specific, measurable, attainable, realistic, and tangible, in other words, SMART. In every aspect of your life, goal setting will play a role in determining whether you succeed or you fail. More than 90% of people do not have goals, they just go about life one day at a time.

While setting SMART goals is a step in the right direction, it can only get you so far. You still have to supplement them with other techniques to make sure that you succeed, and this is where neuro-linguistic programming comes in handy. You might have penned your ideas on paper, but are you mentally ready to challenge what lies ahead? Meeting goals is about more than just ticking things off your checklist, it is also about changing behaviors and attitudes. It is about believing in yourself, and the fact that you can change your situation.

What are goals?

People keep talking about goals and setting goals, but you wonder whether they know what they are talking about. What are goals? Goals are the end result, something you work to achieve. There are different types of goals, primary and secondary. Primary goals are the things that you want to achieve, while secondary goals are the things that you have to achieve to meet the primary goals.

Goals can be powerful, especially when you are passionate about them, and you have them aligned with your beliefs and attitudes. Beliefs and attitudes are at the center of neuro-linguistic programming. When you have your goals aligned with your personal values, they can become a powerful force in your life, and nothing can stop you from achieving what you want.

One of the best things you learn about goal setting is that it is a never-ending process of discovery. You learn so much about yourself as you strive to set and meet your goals. In the beginning, you might not know what you desire, but as you keep unraveling milestones towards your ultimate goal, some things will become clearer to you. This explains why some people realize the things that they value deeply at a very late stage in life.

There are two ways of setting goals that have proven effective in the past, holistic management and neuro-linguistic programming. Holistic management is about making wise decisions which help you achieve your goals in an effective way. Neuro-linguistic programming, on the other hand, is about making you effective in whichever context you are setting goals in. These methods both have unique tools, and they can spur your personal growth and see you live a comfortable and fulfilling life.

In neuro-linguistic programming, you are encouraged to work towards meeting your goals, not running away from a problem. Problems should not be your end-point. As you make plans, ensure you know the signs to look for, signs that will alert you when you are veering off-course. If what you are doing does not seem to work, there is nothing wrong with trying something else.

Before we delve into how neuro-linguistic programming can help you with goal setting, we must look at how the brain functions. The human brain responds to feelings, sounds, and images. In neuro-linguistic programming, the goal is to help you by making your goals specific to one of these three features. Other than that, you also need to use the right words to give your goals meaning, or you might not be any different than everyone else who never achieve their goals every year.

Through neuro-linguistic programming, you will not just be working towards your goals, you will also be pushing your body and mind towards it. Neuro-linguistic programming introduces a physiological and neurological concept into goal setting.

Neuro-linguistic programming is very specific. It focuses on the things that you can feel, see, or hear, helping you manifest the goals internally. From this, you can move your goals from the current state to your preferred state. The following is a guide on how to use neuro-linguistic programming techniques to set clear and achievable goals:

Positivity in goal setting

Be positive when setting goals. Consider your current situation when planning for what you want to achieve in the future. Think about the things you want to achieve. You can make a list then go through it, making sure you are positive about them.

Specificity

You must give your goals an element of specificity. Consider unique sensory terms that would make your goal specific. For example, how will you feel when you achieve your goals, or what should you see to remind you that you have succeeded?

Outline the steps that you must follow to reach your goals. While describing the process, try to use all your senses so that you can engage the nervous system and your brain. You can start with an overall goal, then narrow it down to smaller milestones that you can achieve. Analyze the milestones to ensure that they are not overwhelming.

Do you feel compelled by the goals you want to achieve? Think about it for a while, and ask yourself whether you feel there is a unique pull to the goals. This is about sharing a connection to your goals.

Goal evaluation

You must aim for wholesome progress when setting goals. Analyze your goals to make sure that achieving them will be perfect for all aspects of your life. Do you feel that by achieving your goals, your personal life will feel complete? What will change in your life once you have accomplished the goals, that you do not have presently? What do you stand to lose in order to meet your goals? These are some of the important questions you need to think about.

The questions you ask here are supposed to help you figure out whether meeting your goals will make your life complete. They also help you actualize the goals, imprinting on your subconscious mind.

Maintenance

Think about the goals that you are working towards, and imagine you have already achieved your targets. Do you think it is possible for you to sustain the progress? More often, goals that you initiate on your own are easier to maintain over the long-term than those that are initiated from external influence.

To understand this concept, ask yourself whether you feel you are in control of the goals and if you achieve them, whether you have the power in you to make it. Wholesome goals are supposed to be about you. These are goals that you can maintain. Achieving and maintaining these goals should never depend on someone else being present, or adding their input. Good goals should be a representation of things that are within your control. If that is not the case, and you need someone else's input, then meeting your goals will always be a function of someone else's ideologies, making you no different from a puppet.

Contextualize your goals

Goal setting does not just end at thinking or

writing down what you want to achieve, you must give it context and perspective. How do you plan on getting your goals? Where should you be to achieve it? When do you have to achieve it? With whom will you achieve the goals? Context gets you so far when setting goals. It makes the goals real. You can readjust your goals accordingly until you are satisfied that the context is suitable.

Resource allocation

Consider goal setting to be like any other project you are working on. Think about the resources you need to allocate for it. What do you need for you to meet your goals? Do you have all the necessary resources? Do you need more? Are there some resources that are not within your reach? Do you know anyone else who has achieved the same goals you are working towards? If so, talk to them about it, and find out what their journey was like.

In all these steps, the most important thing is for you to know when you have realized your goals.

This is why you need a plan. Without a plan, how will you know you have met your goals?

Goal setting through neuro-linguistic programming

It is true that not everyone lives the life that they desire or the one they want. This is quite unfortunate because it also means that someone else plans their lives with you as a pawn in it, and you get to live your life according to their plans. That aside, there is always something that you feel you do not have, but can work harder or change something in your environment to get it. It could be something nice, or something you have always dreamt of. The human brain is programmed to strive for more, and this is why we are predisposed to work towards happiness.

You must be specific to have a shot at getting the things you want. Specificity in neuro-linguistic programming is a part of well-formedness. These are conditions that you meet and find it easier to achieve your goals. The moment you are happy and satisfied with your goal setting, you will have a well-formed goal.

One of the key tenets of neuro-linguistic programming in goal setting is for you to have a clear and concise outcome plan. If you do not know what you want, it becomes difficult for you to get there. With the outcome, you check to make sure it aligns with your personality, with who you are. Once you are aware of this, you use the feedback you receive to determine how to change your behavior, beliefs, and attitudes to help you meet your goals. The neuro-linguistic programming approach to goal setting, therefore, focuses on the outcome, your awareness, and your flexibility in changing perspectives, and your behavior patterns.

A well-formed outcome must meet certain conditions to satisfy you. This is where you start when mapping your goals. Experts advise that when setting goals, you should always start with the outcome. You can state the outcomes you are working towards in different ways. However, there are some basics that must feature in the said outcomes.

You have to state the outcomes in a positive way. The outcome should be stated as what you want to achieve, and not what you do not want. You must also make sure that you are working towards something that you can control.

Importance of brainstorming in goal setting

You might come to a point where you are unable to proceed without talking to someone. Neuro-linguistic programming encourages you to reach out to people who might share the same sentiments, or who you consider successful in the field you are trying to succeed in. Consulting a mentor can help you understand parts of your goal setting that are undefined, vague, or the ones that might be problematic for you.

Brainstorming also allows you the chance to see your goals from the perspective of someone who has been there and done it all. You get the benefit of seeing your goals from a different point of view. They can also share with you some possible scenarios of how your goals might play out, so you have lots of options to work with. It can be quite the eye-opener. Talking to someone who has achieved what you are working towards can help you fine-tune your goals, and create the dream that you have always wanted.

One important lesson you will learn from brainstorming is the need to commit to your goals. Commitment goes a long way in helping you meet the expected outcome. Your goals only work to the extent that you want them to. How far are you willing to push yourself to achieve your goals?

Chapter 14: Challenges and Limitations of Neuro-Linguistic Programming

Neuro-linguistic programming requires discipline. It is impossible for most agencies and individuals to discipline themselves without an external authority being involved. The concept of discipline is rather simple – any discipline must find a way of disciplining itself, or it might wither off into oblivion, ceasing to exist.

While neuro-linguistic programming has been touted in the past to help with a variety of issues in daily communication, there are challenges that bog this field. In the US, there does not exist a distinct community around neuro-linguistic programming. This raises a lot of questions concerning the progress of neuro-linguistic programming as a whole. In light of concerns that some neurology experts have had in the past, there is limited academic progress in neuro-linguistic programming. It is easy to see this as a challenge, but it is also a call to action, for experts to keep studying neuro-linguistic programming and usher the study into the future.

Hypothetical Observations

One of the major criticisms that have been leveled against neuro-linguistic programming in the past is that most, if not all of the observations that were made in the study are hypothetical. A hypothesis should never be taken as proof of something. A hypothesis should be used as the foundation upon which scientific research and studies will be conducted.

A lot of the underlying models that have been proposed in neuro-linguistic programming have barely held their fort in the face of scientific scrutiny. To make things worse, it is not easy to come across peer-reviewed research or journals that support the neuro-linguistic programming techniques. On the contrary, a lot of reviews and articles have sprung up over the years, challenging the models proposed in neuro-linguistic programming.

Lack of Awareness

The field of neuro-linguistic programming lacks recognition and awareness, compared to most of the other fields of study. There are not so many credible forums discussing neuro-linguistic programming where you can find relatable discussions. Because of this, it is not always easy to come across open discussions about the benefits or disadvantages of neuro-linguistic programming.

Credibility is lacking, especially since no credible journal has addressed the weaknesses or strengths of neuro-linguistic programming. As a study, neuro-linguistic programming does have limitations, which the adherents are yet to admit.

Terminology

One of the biggest peeves for neuro-linguistic programming is the terminology used around it. The term *programming* is often misconstrued by most people to involve computing. However, much reframing can be done to this term, it is almost impossible to convince someone who is averse to computers and computing that neuro-linguistic programming is not about manipulation into nothing more than a computer bot.

There have been recommendations to change it from programming to psychology, though this is yet to bear any fruit. A lot of people worry about the rapid effect of neuro-linguistic programming. If you are able to change phobias in an individual in a few minutes, what else are you able to do to them without their knowledge? These are some of the concerns that make it difficult for some people to accept neuro-linguistic programming, especially the potential for manipulation.

Besides, the concept of seeing the brain as a computer is an old assessment that has since been disapproved in modern psychological studies. Today experts view the brain as a network, complete with information processing concepts and nodes. While the computing theory as proposed by *Grinder* and *Bandler* back in the day was innovative and made a lot of sense, these concepts have been overtaken by time, research, and innovative technology. Neuroscience evidence, in particular, disapproves this idea, in light of tangible evidence from research into different aspects of neuroscience.

Manipulation

There is always the risk of manipulation with neuro-linguistic programming. As a patient, you should get into an alternate reality at your own pace and on your terms. However, many are the times when experts force patients into alternate realities. This level of manipulation is bound to make someone think twice about neuro-linguistic programming.

The other challenge that comes with manipulation is that most people are aware of how powerful neuro-linguistic programming can be. For this reason, some patients will barely put in the effort when they come to visit an expert.

They expect a miracle. It is this kind of arrogance that further makes it difficult for neuro-linguistic programming experts to practice.

Lack of Growth

The study of neuro-linguistic programming has been a stub for a long time. It appears that neuro-linguistic programming has been stagnant. Over the years, there have been major milestones and advancement in neuroscience, cognitive sciences, information processing theories, and social psychology.

While these studies have advanced and changed over the course of time, neuro-linguistic programming has stagnated. Neuro-linguistic programming supporters barely change, test, or challenge the earlier theories and models that were advanced years ago. The same school of thought that was introduced more than 5 decades ago is what is being fronted in neuro-linguistic programming classes.

It is important that neuro-linguistic

programming embraces new developments in research, and incorporates the vast richness of technology to strengthen, reinforce, and debunk some of the observations and theories that have been fronted in the past on neuro-linguistic programming.

Clinical Value

A lot of the techniques that were proposed for neuro-linguistic programming do not have a basis for clinical value. There are very few techniques that are proposed for neuro-linguistic programming. Unfortunately, most of these techniques cannot stand the test of clinical trials. As a result, they cannot make any credible changes to individual behavior.

In the heat of the moment, these techniques can, at best, influence an individual's behavior, but they fail to address the key underlying reasons behind the behavior traits that the individual is expressing. This is more like treating symptoms instead of addressing the reason why someone is sick.

Based on this assessment, therefore, neuro-linguistic programming techniques might not be effective when used on their own. They must be used alongside other techniques if they are to be useful. However, for a field of study that has been stagnant for a long time, this intellectual fusion seems rather unlikely.

Need for Intention

It is highly unlikely that you will experience any progress if you engage in neuro-linguistic programming for the sake of it. Experts recommend intention for neuro-linguistic programming to be effective. The patient has to be determined to realize the changes they need to see in their lives for this to work.

Many are those who have used neuro-linguistic programming to quit smoking, but they did not have the desire to quit in the first place. This leaves them at a loss, and some eventually revert to their former behavior. For the therapist, dealing with a patient who is not committed to making the changes in their lives can be a problem.

It is impossible for the therapist to determine what you want, and help you achieve it without you going the extra mile. As a patient, you must put in a lot of work. Your desire for change will be key to the success of neuro-linguistic programming. You must come prepared. Preparation means you get your head in the right frame, fully aware of what you expect from the neuro-linguistic programming session.

Limited academic research

One of the challenges facing neuro-linguistic programming as a study is that there is very little academic research or publishing that has been done in the field. There are lots of sporadic studies that have been done on neuro-linguistic programming. Most of these are offshoots of studies into other fields that share a few similarities with neuro-linguistic programming, such as training and development, neuroscience and meditation.

Most of the publications of neuro-linguistic programming are done by individuals who are deep in the neuro-linguistic programming community, so this opens very little room for criticism from outside.

Conclusion

Neuro-linguistic programming is an interesting field of study. We have discussed a number of disciplines that most people relate to almost every single day of their lives. Neuro-linguistic programming is about turning your life around, making changes in life that will get you going places.

There are a lot of things that we take for granted, but this is not supposed to be the case. Awareness about people and the environment around us is an important skill, espoused in emotional intelligence. You have to know what people are dealing with, and why they are behaving the way they do.

For people who are in management, neuro-linguistic programming is a process that will change your perception of your employees and the teams you work with. It gives you tools that enable you to interact better with them. For your employees, your awareness and sensitivity to their feelings go a long way. It inspires confidence in them about your role as their leader, and they are more willing to work with you.

Neuro-linguistic programming teaches you skills and techniques that are useful not just at work, but in different spheres of your life. The skills you learn can help you rebuild your personal relationships, and even save a relationship that is on its deathbed. One of the challenges that most people struggle with is communication. It is not just in the words they speak, but the meanings that they attach to those words.

You learn to mean what you say in neuro-linguistic programming because integrity and sincerity go a long way in making someone understand your message. You learn to hear, see, and feel communication in the words that people speak, the facial expressions and the gestures that they make while you are at it. These are some of the things that make a big difference between successful communication and failed communication.

You might not have realized it yet, but communication takes place around you all the time. Communication forms the basis of interaction at all levels. Even when people are not talking, there is some form of communication going on, and you can read this by your awareness of the non-verbal cues.

Learning about neuro-linguistic programming gets you closer to achieving your goals. You might have already figured out your plans, but working towards them is a different ball game. When you are mapping your goals, it is important that you consider them from a wholesome point of view. Through neuro-linguistic programming, you will learn how to conceptualize your goals, and internalize them. This is also an aspect that you learn through meditation, so by learning neuro-linguistic programming, you will improve your chances of success with meditation and positive affirmations.

A lot of people struggle with stress at different times in their lives. Stress is consuming and can turn your life into a nightmare if you do not manage it well. If you are stressed and do not manage it well, chances are high that you could lose control, and find yourself struggling to keep your life together. Stress has also been linked to a lot of medical concerns, like high cholesterol, blood pressure, and heart problems. Managing stress is one of the things you can do to live a long and fruitful life.

While it is normal to see the negative side of things, neuro-linguistic programming teaches you that there could be some benefits of a bit of stress in your life. What you will learn, however, is that you could use a bit of stress in your life, to push you and make you do amazing things in life. Stress pushes you out of your comfort zone and gets you thinking about better ways of doing things.

Struggling with phobia or overcoming a traumatic event in life? You can overcome this through neuro-linguistic programming. We train our minds to focus on the negative aspects of life so much, to the point where the negativity consumes us. The human brain is elastic and has an insane limit when it comes to the things you can learn. Just in the same way that you learn to remember negative experiences, you can also change them into positive ones, to help you overcome your emotional challenges.

There is no limit to the things that you can achieve when you master the neuro-linguistic programming techniques and skills. Some skills might require the assistance of an expert, but most of the techniques are things that you can do on your own.

One of the most important lessons that you learn in neuro-linguistic programming is that you are the change you want to see in your life. Everything that you want to achieve in this life is within your grasp. You just need to challenge for it and make it yours. If you are a leader, you will learn useful tips that can help you manage your teams well, communicate with them, and get them working towards accomplishing your overall goals.

Neuro-linguistic programming is an essential part of growth and development, whether you are going for personal or professional growth. You can refine your life, your experiences and your perceptions by being receptive to changing behaviors, beliefs, and attitudes, and all this is possible through neuro-linguistic programming.

www.ingramcontent.com/pod-product-compliance
Lightning Source LLC
Chambersburg PA
CBHW030110100526
44591CB00009B/353